American Liturgy

American Liturgy

*Finding Theological Meaning
in the Holy Days of US Culture*

James Calvin Davis

CASCADE *Books* · Eugene, Oregon

AMERICAN LITURGY
Finding Theological Meaning in the Holy Days of US Culture

Cascade Books
An Imprint of Wipf and Stock Publishers
199 W. 8th Ave., Suite 3
Eugene, OR 97401

www.wipfandstock.com

PAPERBACK ISBN: 978-1-7252-7131-9
HARDCOVER ISBN: 978-1-7252-7130-2
EBOOK ISBN: 978-1-7252-7132-6

Cataloguing-in-Publication data:

Names: Davis, James Calvin, author.

Title: American liturgy : finding theological meaning in the holy days of US culture / James Calvin Davis.

Description: Eugene, OR: Cascade Books, 2021 | Includes bibliographical references and index.

Identifiers: ISBN 978-1-7252-7131-9 (paperback) | ISBN 978-1-7252-7130-2 (hardcover) | ISBN 978-1-7252-7132-6 (ebook)

Subjects: LCSH: Holidays—United States. | Festivals—United States. | United States—Social life and customs.

Classification: GT 4803 .D3 2021 (paperback) | GT 4803 (ebook)

02/09/21

For Mom and Dad,
and in gratitude for the life of
Russell C. Carpenter (1941–2020)

Contents

ORDINARY TIME

Acknowledgments

I am grateful to Rodney Clapp and the other kind folks at Cascade Books for their confidence in this project and for editorial support along the way, especially in a publishing season made more complicated (to say the least) by the COVID-19 pandemic. I also wish to thank my home institution, Middlebury College, for a sabbatical that allowed me to complete this book. Middlebury remains a fitting laboratory for considering intersections between Christian conviction and secular culture, and for twenty years it has been a wonderful place from which to be a "public theologian."

My spouse, Elizabeth, copyedited my entire manuscript, as she has done with every book I have written. I have grown dependent on her services, and my publishers have benefited unwittingly too! I know this book is more elegant because she offers that aid generously, with no complaint (and with no discernible reward). For her professional expertise and loving partnership, I give thanks publicly once again. Our two sons, Jae and Kisung, have grown accustomed to seeing their names in print in my books, so I will thank them here for regular reminders that there is more to life than writing theology. Things like football, of course.

This book would not exist at all without the influence of my home congregation, the Congregational Church of Middlebury, Vermont, where I serve as theologian-in-residence. Many of these essays began as sermons preached in their midst, and for eight years my delightful church friends have tolerated the insufferable Presbyterian hanging out with them, engaging me in conversations that have consistently sharpened my thinking. I am truly blessed to be part of such a thoughtful, faithful, theologically invested, and fun-loving group of people. I am especially grateful for our dedicated

Monday Evening Adult Study Group, a community of people with a strange enthusiasm for thinking theologically about the world in which we live and serve. I need to recognize in a special way Charles and Nancy Jakiela, two church friends who insisted at regular intervals that the sermons and classes I share at church make their way to print. I happily blame them for the existence of this book.

This volume is dedicated to the memory of Russell Carpenter, the longtime moderator of our congregation, who died unexpectedly in February 2020. In his role as moderator, Russ paved the way for me to become theologian-in-residence, but he also was a cherished friend with an infectious laugh and, as universally acclaimed at his packed memorial service, a man of rare Christian character. We miss you, Russ.

This book is also offered in honor of my parents, Bill and Kathy Davis. I am overdue to dedicate one of my books to them, given their impact on the person I have become and the vocation I am trying to fulfill. Without their labor and care, I likely would not have escaped the challenging economic circumstances in which I was raised to attend college. Without their insistence on church as the center of our family life, the call to preaching and teaching would have been more difficult to discern. And without the influence of their worldviews, the perspective on theology and American culture captured in this book would be shallower indeed. Mom may not approve of the chapter on swearing, but otherwise I trust they are proud of what I have done here, and I hope they see their fingerprints all over it. For their love and investment, I give thanks to God.

Introduction

Christian Theology and American Culture

How can celebrating the "holy days" of American culture inform the relationship between Christian faith and American identity? Mother's Day, Independence Day, Super Bowl Sunday, and other cultural holidays of various origins have become part of the way Americans tell time. These holidays mark our collective progression through each year, while encouraging us to revisit values and practices that we associate with national life. Some of these holidays reflect the Christian heritage of the United States, while others are primarily patriotic in their reference. Some of the holy days of American culture reflect seasonal activities, like summer vacations and the resumption of school in the fall. Observing these holy days of culture has been important to our sense of national identity, ritual markers of an American civil religion.

For a variety of reasons, I think it is appropriate for Christians to reflect theologically on the meaning in these cultural celebrations. Obviously American Christians live in the intersection of two identities, so that faithful participation in both religious community and nation requires that we think about how the two loyalties complement and challenge one another. Reflection on the rituals of national life through the lens of Christian belief invites us to consider the relationship between related but distinct sets of values. Are there ways in which the rituals of national life mark a kind of "idolatry" that pulls us away from the central convictions of Christian faith? In what ways might Christian convictions critique or deepen our participation in national culture? Are there values in the rituals of the American calendar that complement or constructively critique our practice of Christian values?

1

Christian theology and the holy days of American culture often come together in Sunday worship, as preachers across the country regularly offer sermons on Father's Day, Labor Day, Thanksgiving, and other holidays, sermons that attempt a connection between Christian convictions and cultural themes. Unfortunately, my experience has been that many of these attempts peddle in simplistic associations that take one of two forms: either an insufficiently critical baptism of cultural celebrations or an equally superficial hostility toward "the culture" in favor of more "authentic" Christian values. My hope is that the essays in this book offer a more nuanced alternative than those two options. Some of these essays view the holy days of the American calendar through the lens of Christian faith to reveal shortcomings in our culture. Other essays will use a cultural holiday to challenge how the church practices its faith. Still other essays will suggest ways in which Christian and cultural values cooperate to call our attention to something authentic and good. Many of the essays will try to do more than one of these things. Together I hope they will help preachers and laypeople think with theological subtlety about the connections and disconnect between being Christian and being American.

THINKING THEOLOGICALLY

Perhaps a book that encourages Christians to think theologically about aspects of culture ought to make clear what it means to "think theologically." In my last book, I offered this definition of Christian theology: "Christian theology is the collective project of understanding ourselves, the human community, the world, and the cosmos in relation to God, through the interpretive lens of what Jesus Christ reveals to us about God and in conversation with the best sources of knowledge available in our time and place."[1] A couple of things are important about this understanding of theology. First, the aim of theology is to help us relate our experience of the worlds we inhabit to God, as we know God to be revealed in Jesus Christ. That means that Jesus' testament to God becomes paramount to making sense of not just our religious lives, but our social, cultural, moral, and political interactions with members of all the other communities in which we participate (human and otherwise). Of course, Christians disagree about what is most important to draw from Jesus' ministry for our understanding of God and our obligations to God. This means the work of interpretation is essential. No single understanding of God falls out of the biblical stories of Christ and his significance, so Christians owe it to themselves and the broader church

---

1. Davis, *Forbearance*, 6.

to do the work of interpretation, to learn more about how others past and present have understood Jesus Christ and his ministry, and to discuss and debate with one another about which interpretations of Christ's revelation of God ought to strike us as most compelling.

This is hard work, and it is the work of the whole church. Christian theology is not an individual experience to be privatized with the secrecy of the ballot box. Christian theology is not just a personal belief system but a collective endeavor, because theology is the language of the whole church. Neither is theology the domain of a specialized group. To be sure, some members of the Christian community may be specially trained in biblical studies, historical studies, systematic thinking, or ethical analysis, and we certainly should avail ourselves of that expertise. But doing the theology of the church is not a chore we simply relegate to those with advanced degrees. The task of theology ultimately belongs to the whole church, because it is our collective expression of the witness of Jesus Christ to the worlds we inhabit.

Finally, theology requires us to think expansively, understanding ourselves in the widest contexts possible. This is not to dismiss the importance of particular communities as the context for theological reflection. The best Christian theologies of justice being written today originate from the perspective of historically marginalized communities, arguing that the experience of oppression and injustice itself is a source of God's revelation. Good theology thinks seriously about the particular experiences that shape its starting point, but good theology also commits to moving beyond local, tribal, and national communities to consider our relation to God and others in global, ecological, even cosmic contexts. To do so is to imagine the universe with God as its center, rather than our own clan or species. That theocentric commitment is, to my mind, the most faithful rendition of a basic Christian confession: God is the Alpha and the Omega, the beginning and the end.[2]

This theocentric perspective is a chief characteristic of the subtradition in Christian theology with which I identify and which you will see reflected in these essays: *Reformed* theology. The easiest way to define Reformed theology is to say it is a tradition that draws on the intellectual heritage of the Protestant Reformer John Calvin. This is a family lineage that includes English and American Puritans, Jonathan Edwards, Friedrich Schleiermacher, and Charles Hodge. More recently it includes Karl Barth, the Niebuhr brothers, James Gustafson, Allen Boesak, Katie Cannon, Douglas Ottati, and Cynthia Rigby. Theologians within this tradition respect and

---

2. My emphasis on a theocentric perspective is undoubtedly influenced by the work of James M. Gustafson, especially his epic *Ethics from a Theocentric Perspective*.

build from the work of thinkers before them, but they are not excessively or exclusively beholden to them.

What they draw from this tradition, and what binds them to it, are certain themes. Reformed theology begins with belief in the ultimate sovereignty of God, by which Reformed thinkers mean the conviction that God is the Creator, Redeemer, and Sustainer of the entire cosmos. This emphasis on God's sovereignty contrasts with relegations of God's relevance to private spirituality or the experience of one group of people over and against others. In Reformed theology, the God whom Christians worship is the God of the whole cosmos. Reformed theology also takes seriously the reality of sin as an important dimension to the human condition. Sin is a serious impediment to knowing what is good and doing what is right, and it is rooted in something deeper than mere ignorance. Sin is a self-defeating penchant that is "hardwired" into individuals and communities, and it manifests itself in human tendencies like pride, inordinate self-regard, and the abuse of power. As an antidote to this human condition, Reformed theology emphasizes the necessity of divine grace for the redemption of the world. In contrast to theologies that suggest human beings must merit salvation by doing good things or following God's laws, Reformed theology insists human beings are reconciled to God through the initiative of God's grace alone. This is not to say human effort is irrelevant to the life of faith, but for the Reformed tradition our efforts to do good are properly understood as grateful response to the God who first reaches out to us. The result is a Reformed vision of piety in which gratitude is lived in and for the world. Instead of withdrawing from a world considered dangerous to faithfulness, Reformed Christians express their gratitude for divine grace by living faithfully in the world, and in doing so testify to the goodness of God, who offers the gift of reconciliation to the world.

These are some of the theological themes that draw the Reformed Christian tradition together; you will see them at work in many of the essays that follow. Reformed theology bases its understanding of this grand narrative of grace in the Bible. The Bible is the reliable testament to the character and intentions of God, who is revealed decisively in the person and ministry of Jesus Christ. You also will see regular appeals to sources beyond the Bible in these essays, which discloses another important feature of my theology. An unapologetic embrace of other sources of insight besides Scripture marks my theology as *liberal*, and I proudly embrace that label. Liberal theology takes seriously the wisdom we glean from science, philosophy, history, rational reflection, and the experience of individuals and communities. It sees this wisdom as opportunity to confirm or revise what the Christian tradition has said about a whole host of topics. For instance, modern science invites us to subscribe to a geological understanding of the world that is different than the one reflected in the biblical texts. The experience of women compels us to critique and correct Christianity's preoccupation with men's power and perspective. History helps us to understand the commonalities and differences between discrete episodes in the Christian story. Philosophy reminds us that there is wisdom to be found beyond the Christian tradition that can deepen or correct theological claims. A hallmark of liberal theology is that these other sources of insight are no threat to the integrity of Christian believing, and in fact they often contribute constructively to Christian theology by helping us distinguish traditional convictions that remain authentic and useful from those that ought to be revised or set aside in our time and place. To appeal to sources beyond the Bible is to affirm faith in a sovereign God who is powerful enough to speak through conduits other than Scripture.

Liberal theology also takes seriously that human communities are products of history, so both the biblical authors' and our own understandings of God and the world are affected by time and place. As a result, we should not be surprised when the passage of time requires some adjustment in understanding, even an understanding that is reflected in the Bible. None of this is to say that the past is *always* disposable. Rather it is to suggest that good theology engages Scripture and tradition in a bidirectional relationship of reflection with other sources of insight, allowing the wisdom of the past and the knowledge of the present to inform, challenge, and revise one another. As Christians we measure the authenticity of this bidirectional reflection against what we know to be true about God as revealed to us in the person and ministry of Jesus Christ. To engage in this theological exercise is to live into a mantra for which the Reformed tradition is well known, a commitment to a church that is "reformed and always reforming."

This openness to a bidirectional relationship of influence between the past and the present and between the Bible and other sources of insight distinguishes my theology from many so-called conservative Christian theologies, in which authority is recognized as flowing only one way. In the effort to literally conserve the past, conservative Christian theologies demand that the principal authority for the life of faith is Scripture, and all other sources of knowledge must conform to or be revised according to that authority. This categorical deference to Scripture is often accompanied by an allegedly literal reading of the Bible, and the claim is that there is a timelessness to scriptural witness from which we cannot deviate without challenge to the authority of the Bible.

Of course, the claim to timelessness ignores the reality that the Bible was inspired by God but written by human hands. Those human writers

existed in time, and their understanding of God's word reflects their context. So it is with current-day conservative Christians who read the Bible;
their reading of what is "literally" in the Bible also reflects the influence
of their time and place, whether they admit it or not (and they often do
not). Reading the Bible as signaling a clear preference for democracy, or
an endorsement of capitalism, or an unambiguous condemnation of abortion betrays the influence of modern American values and preoccupations
onto the exercise of biblical interpretation. Neither democratic governance
nor capitalist systems nor modern scientific understandings of fetal development were ideas known to the biblical writers. Conservative Christians
interpret the Bible just like liberal Christians, and in interpreting the Bible,
conservatives read it through the prism of two millennia of Christian tradition and through the influence of their own time and contexts, just like
liberal Christians. There is no such thing as reading Scripture without interpreting it, and there is no way to interpret Scripture in a historical or
cultural vacuum. Put sharply, the classic byline of classical Reformers, *sola
scriptura* (Scripture only), is the great Protestant lie! The difference between
conservative Christian theologies and liberal ones is not that the former
respect the authority of the Bible and the latter do not. Both conservative
and liberal theologies interpret the Bible in their historical context and are
influenced by insights and values gleaned from sources beyond the scriptural texts. The difference is that conservative theologies often deny that this
is what they are doing, and liberal theologies usually celebrate it.

To be open to revised interpretations of the Bible and Christian tradition is not to say that the Bible and classical Christian teachings lack authority, and it does not mean that the newest information we have is always
the likeliest to be true and accurate. This last point is an important one to
make in response to some contemporary Christian liberals. Some liberal
Christian theologians write as if no perspective older than the twentieth
century is relevant, for what could it possibly offer to the consideration of
modern social justice issues with which Christian liberals are preoccupied?
In fact, some liberal theologians define a liberal approach as *beginning* with
the rejection of traditional sources.[3] The popular disregard for anything old

3. For one example, see Spong, *Why Christianity Must Change or Die*. See also Gary
Dorrien's definition of liberal theology in *Making of American Liberal Theology*, 3:2–3.
While I agree with Dorrien that liberal theology historically "reconceptualizes the
meaning of Christianity in the light of modern knowledge and ethical values," is "re-
formist in spirit and substance," and is committed "to the authority of individual reason
and experiences," I think he says too much when he suggests that a rejection of "external authority" is essentially part of the liberal tradition. Liberal theology decentral-
izes Scripture and tradition, insisting that these sources of insight share authority with
reason and experience, and for *some* liberal theologians this amounts to the rejection

among liberals is the reason I have less and less use for the term *progressive* as a description of my own theology. In many circles, "liberal" and "progressive" are used interchangeably, but the word *progressive* implies that what comes next is better than what came before. Christian progressives often pride themselves on disregarding tradition as archaic and irrelevant, declaring (as my local Unitarian Universalist church advertises) to value "today's questions . . . more than yesterday's answers."

That assumption may be a common move for so-called progressive theologies, but its historical nearsightedness offends not just the Christian historian but also the humanist in me. Anyone who studies literature, history, philosophy, or art knows that more recent specimens are not necessarily more beautiful or wiser than the old. Should we prefer Barber over Beethoven because the former is more recent? Is Lockean political philosophy irrelevant to modern debates because it was written centuries ago? Ancient texts and art offer wisdom and elegance that can betray the shallow pedestrianism of more modern work. Theology is no different. Students of Christian thought know that classical theology is a treasure trove of wisdom. While our theological ancestors may not have anticipated all the problems we encounter in the modern age, they wrestled with concerns of their own that often serve as useful analogues to ours. The psalmist conveys an angst about suffering that still speaks to people struggling with trauma today. In the sixteenth century, John Calvin wrote with nuance about the gifts and limits of medical science in a way that offers helpful insight to modern Christians who are wrestling with the moral implications of medical technologies he could not even imagine. In the seventeenth century, the Puritan Roger Williams wrote about conscientious freedom and the relationship between religion and state with a complexity and realism that relatively few modern philosophers have matched. In the eighteenth century, Jonathan Edwards wrote about virtue and beauty with such sophistication that he remains one of America's most profound intellectuals. Scripture and classical theology often speak a word of wisdom to us across the ages, and often that wisdom surpasses our own attempts at depth and discernment.

To my mind, good liberal theology feels free to revise tradition when warranted, but it also honors the tradition in which it stands. Indeed, liberal theology itself *is* a tradition, a vein in Christian theology with history and legacy. The tradition of liberal theology consists of a family of thinkers who share a commitment to understanding the historic tenets of the faith in conversation with the best of modern knowledge. Friedrich

---

or near rejection of traditional sources of authority altogether. The abandonment of Scripture and tradition as authorities is not a uniform feature of all liberal theologies, however, as I hope my own demonstrates.

Schleiermacher, Vida Scudder, Walter Rauschenbusch, Howard Thurman, Reinhold Niebuhr, Paul Tillich, Martin Luther King Jr., Rosemary Radford Reuther, Rufus Burrow, Sallie McFague, and Catherine Keller represent just a few thinkers in the great cloud of witnesses who belong to the tradition of liberal theology.[4] And liberal theology can claim antecedent ideas that are even older—for example, the inherent dignity of persons, the importance of reason for religious and moral insight, liberation from injustice, and human rights are all ideals that liberal Christian theologians root deep in theological tradition.[5] The liberal Reformed theology at work in this book makes regular reference to wise thinkers in the broad Christian tradition, even in the effort to say a new thing about contemporary American culture.

THEOLOGICAL INSIGHTS ON, IN, AND FROM CULTURE

The bidirectional reflection between the old and the new is a feature of my theology, and it also influences how I think about culture itself. The term *culture* is notoriously ambiguous, connoting everything from art and literature to social conventions. I am using it here to refer to the practices, systems, habits, assumptions, and values by which a community defines itself. A society's culture consists of its history and the values it draws from that history, even that part of its history that is contested. Culture consists of traditions that symbolize and reinforce a community's values, including the traditions of time (that is, calendars and holidays). High art and literature are vehicles of culture, but so are popular media, politics, and civic practices. Culture is not static; it is a dynamic confrontation between a community's history and its present, as both the defenders and opponents of Confederate monuments in the South know too well. It is subject to challenge and reinterpretation, including identifying aspects of a community's history that the community no longer finds worthy of celebration, or discovering voices in that community's history heretofore stifled but worthy of elevation. Culture is the interplay between a society's dominant memory and, in Emilie Townes's evocative term, the "countermemory" of the society's marginalized and forgotten.[6] In this way, culture is a dynamic collective experience, lived out in its traditions and practices, of identifying, reinforcing, challenging, and changing the values for which it stands, and thereby symbolizing

---

4. For the rich intellectual history of this Christian sub-tradition, see Dorrien, *Making of American Liberal Theology* and Langford, *Tradition of Liberal Theology*.

5. Langford, *Tradition of Liberal Theology*, 1–9.

6. Townes, *Womanist Ethics and the Cultural Production of Evil*, 21–27.

who it is as community. To belong in such a society is to participate in the traditions and practices of culture.

The United States has a culture—dynamic and contested traditions, practices, and histories that together represent a national identity. Many of these practices and values are symbolized in the holidays featured in this book. Like other sources of insight, the values and media of contemporary American culture can be a help or a hindrance to thinking and living faithfully as a Christian. In many pulpits in the United States, however, "the culture" is routinely demonized as the moral enemy of Christian conviction. Turn on any of the religious broadcasting networks on your TV and you will invariably hear a megachurch pastor thundering about the anti-Christian temptations that lurk in the culture around us. Popular music encourages sexual promiscuity, while TV shows propagate violence and homosexuality. Political culture threatens the nuclear family, while modern literature encourages juvenile delinquency and anarchy. The culture is a cesspool of deviance against which faith is a bulwark, if only Christians remain vigilant.

In his classic book *Christ and Culture*, H. Richard Niebuhr identified several different patterns that Christians historically have adopted for thinking about the intersection of church and culture. He called the one I am describing now "Christ against culture."[7] Since its earliest days, the church sometimes has defined the life of faith over and against the culture around it. From this perspective, the church is a community founded on radically different values than the culture around it. The world's culture reflects moral standards and priorities of a profane world that does not know Christ or God's expectations for humanity. But the church is the fellowship of believers who, in their call to the way of Christ, have taken on new standards for behavior that mark them as distinct from the world around them. In this oppositional framework, the church has a responsibility to stay true to the expectations of Christ and to avoid the pollution of the world. Holiness and purity are goods that the church is called to maintain, in part by limiting its exposure to the temptations of the world around it. These days this oppositional understanding of culture is especially prevalent in American evangelicalism, though it also shows up in the work of the late Pope John Paul II and among disciples of Stanley Hauerwas.

This oppositional understanding of church and culture can be rooted in the Bible, especially in the New Testament Epistles. For instance, in 2 Corinthians 6, Paul cautions the Christian community in Corinth, "Do not be mismatched with unbelievers. For what partnership is there between righteousness and lawlessness?" He characterizes the difference between

7. Niebuhr, *Christ and Culture*, ch. 2.

church and culture as the distinction between light and darkness, and suggests that separating from the idolatry of culture is part of the calling to be God's people:

> For we are the temple of the living God; as God said,
> "I will live in them and walk among them,
> and I will be their God, and they shall be my people.
> Therefore come out from them, and be separate from them, says
> the Lord." (2 Cor 6:16b–17a)

Similarly the writer of 2 Peter suggests God gives Christians the promises and power necessary to "escape the corruption that is in the world because of lust," so that we "may become participants of the divine nature" (1:4). But that comes with a corresponding responsibility to take on the virtues of holiness and to live distinctly in the world. Finally, 1 John 2:15–17 directly warns its readers that love of God and love of the world are not compatible:

> Do not love the world or the things in the world. The love of the
> Father is not in those who love the world; for all that is in the
> world—the desire of the flesh, the desire of the eyes, the pride in
> riches—comes not from the Father but from the world. And the
> world and its desire are passing away, but those who do the will
> of God live forever.

From the perspective represented in these biblical passages, the relationship between church and culture is one of opposition, and the church must remain vigilant against the intrusion of cultural values into the church and the seduction of idolatry that comes from the world.

There are plenty of times when a critical stance against culture seems right to me, though I suspect my favorite critiques of culture will differ from those of conservative TV preachers. For me, entrenched racism, the continued objectification of women, the moral numbness with which we ignore atrocities around immigration, and the destructive tenor of political discourse in the United States are the most glaring examples of cultural tendencies against which the church ought to stand in strong opposition. Feminist theologian Kristine Culp argues that part of the task of theology is to discern when culture is corrupt and idolatrous, and in those moments the church is called to stand up against the culture in a spirit of resistance.[8]

But, consistent with my liberal theological orientation, I think culture can be a good thing too, a source of insight that sometimes complements and confirms what Christian principles tell us is good and right. This more

---

8. Culp, "Always Reforming, Always Resisting," 153.

positive approach to culture is rooted in theological conviction as well, namely the belief that human culture is a gift from God and a conduit through which the sovereign God can reveal wisdom to us. When thinking about art and sculpture, for instance, John Calvin readily admitted that culture is a gift of God and thus can have legitimate and positive use. He also utilized philosophy when he thought it served his theological purposes.[9] Karl Barth was unwilling to write theology without a good dose of Mozart and the newspaper to precede the exercise.[10] Culture can be a gift and complement to Christian theology.

Engagement with culture also is absolutely essential to living the Christian faith in the world, because culture is the "local language" in which we are called to preach and live the gospel. Jesus ate with sinners and went to parties (e.g., Luke 5:29–39), and in doing so we might say he acknowledged that the world and its culture are not something for the church to avoid at all costs, out of some desire to remain pure. Instead, Jesus modeled for the church a proper engagement of culture, to bring the gospel to people by speaking their language and meeting them where they live. Douglas Ottati insists that the church cannot be church without intersecting with culture. "Christians and their communities do not talk about the gospel in general or in the abstract. They talk about it in particular contexts," he writes. "Theologically considered, we should say that they witness of the gospel in response to what God is doing at a particular place and time."[11] Shirley Guthrie reminds us this engagement with culture has been a hallmark of church all along. All the church's historical pronouncements reflect their cultural embeddedness. The creeds and confessions of every age, Guthrie wrote, are shaped by the culture of their times, which gives them a useful "concreteness" as reflections of the concerns of their age, but which also saddles them with inherent "limitations."[12] In other words, creeds and confessions refract and distort "biblical truth" through culture, but as a human endeavor, the church cannot do anything but witness to truth within particular cultures and communities.

Perhaps culture is a mixture of the profane and the good, but the church engages culture in the hope that its presence in the culture will help transform the human community in ways that more closely resemble God's intentions. This is one way to interpret Paul's sermon in Athens, captured in Acts 17:16–34. Paul confronts a city culture that, in his estimation, is lost

9. Calvin, *Institutes*, 112.

10. Green, *Karl Barth*, 322.

11. Ottati, *Hopeful Realism*, 90.

12. Guthrie, *Christian Doctrine*, 24.

and idolatrous. But rather than rejecting it, Paul embraces their practices and traditions in order to transform them. In other words, he uses their culture to draw the Athenians into the gospel of Christ. Here we see biblical precedent for the church to engage culture, neither as an enemy nor as unambiguously good, but as a mission field and a testament to our hope that the world itself will be transformed one day into closer conformity with the gospel. In this way, the church's engagement of culture is a witness to our hope in God's reconciliation.

Besides reinforcing Christian values, though, I think culture from time to time can be a voice of critique against the church, calling the church to catch up to the pace of the moral universe. In our time, marriage equality may be the best example of a front on which culture constructively helped the church move toward its better angels, as shifting trends in cultural comfort with nontraditional relationships clearly influenced many Christian denominations' eventual acceptance of them as well.[13]

I certainly do not mean to suggest that Christianity always should baptize uncritically what is popular in American culture. When cultural trends seem to run counter to Christian values, it presents an opportunity for the church to stand in opposition and contribute to the reformation of public morals. But sometimes cultural values will be consistent with the priorities of Christian living, and other times cultural shifts can signal needed reformation in the church. Consistent with my liberal understanding of theological authenticity, I imagine church and culture in a mutually critical, sometimes complementary, always bidirectional relationship of influence. As Ottati puts it, sometimes we are *against* the culture in our need to prophetically denounce or resist injustices and inhumanities. But more often we are *with* the culture in our common humanity (including common confession of our brokenness), and *for* the culture in our hope that the world will be transformed to God, perhaps in part through our presence in it.[14]

In the essays in this volume, you should expect to see theology and culture interacting in all of these ways. Some of the cultural holy days I feature in this book, for instance, are Christian celebrations in origin, and those essays often will feature an attempt to reclaim the theological significance of those days in the face of cultural tendencies to focus on other, less desirable, things. Some of America's holy days provide us an opportunity to

13. My own denomination, the Presbyterian Church (U.S.A.), is an example of a church that has seemed to be in more of a reactive mode to changing cultural norms around sexuality than a proactive or prophetic one, until recently. Other Protestant denominations, including the United Church of Christ, have been closer to the vanguard of justice for LGBTQ+ persons.

14. Ottati, *Hopeful Realism*, 100.

level Christian theology as a critical lens on values and norms in popular culture. And sometimes our cultural celebrations lend a critical lens to the ways we American Christians practice our faith, calling us to deeper degrees of faithfulness.

In addition to the essays on specific days, I have included chapters on common themes in American culture that do not align perfectly with certain holidays. Because these themes have no association with a specific day, I have grouped them under the title "Ordinary Time," another playful borrowing from the way that historic Christianity tells time, specifically with reference to its calendar between the Lent/Easter and Advent/Christmas celebrations. Themes I explore in this section include profanity, introversion, intolerance, class inequality, and occasions of tragedy. In both the essays prompted by America's holy days and the reflections from our cultural ordinary time, I invite you to think about the ways in which Christian theology can inform our cultural participation and the ways American culture can deepen our faith. Considering the bidirectional influence of faith and culture is an exercise that leads to the improvement of both.

Holy Days

1

The Big Picture

(New Year's Day)

I find myself in a reflective mood as of late, on my way into a year-long sabbatical. For those of us lucky enough to get them, the academic sabbatical gives a teacher time to step away from day-to-day responsibilities in order to do some research and writing, to retool and energize for the classroom, and in general to assess where you have been and where you are going next as a scholar and teacher. On that last front, I find New Year's Day to offer a similar invitation. Never one to get too worked up over watching the ball drop in Times Square, I nonetheless find the new year a helpful opportunity to think about where I have been as a person and a professional over the year being put to bed. The advent of the new year also presents a chance to chart a vision for the future. Those resolutions can become albatrosses around our necks, but more constructively they can help map who and where we want to be twelve months from now.

I have been doing a lot of assessing lately. Since my last sabbatical, I finished up a stint in college administration, made some shifts in my teaching at my college, published a book, started a program at Middlebury called Privilege & Poverty, and performed *lots* of committee work. Life has been interesting and full professionally since my last sabbatical, but the last couple of years have also been hard. For one thing, see the aforementioned college committee work! At home, I have a son who is on the autism spectrum, and it turns out that the cocktail of autism and adolescence is harder to navigate than my spouse Elizabeth and I anticipated, a weight carried by our whole family. In addition, a couple of important relationships have devolved over the last year or so, leaving me feeling a bit used and discarded. With both good and bad to ponder, I find myself embracing this period of reflection as a moment to search for the meaning in it all.

To be honest, I engage in this exercise much more often than annually. For as long as I can remember, on each New Year's Day and many times in between, I have been prone to ask what the "big picture" is in which the experiences of my life ought to make sense. I was born and raised in the Rust Belt of Appalachia, only to find myself later in northern New England. From childhood until well into my graduate studies, I was sure I was called to be a small church pastor, and instead I end up teaching at a secular liberal arts college. Early in our relationship, Elizabeth and I imagined our family one way only to end up exploring the wonderful and challenging world of adoption. Life has been full of unanticipated twists and turns, and I have always been preoccupied with the search for why.

You see, I have never been convinced that simple luck or chance is all there is to how the chapters of life shape and reshape us. And I have seen way too much of the real world to believe for a minute that everything that happens is simply a result of the choices we make. Neither the concept of dumb luck nor the fiction that we are masters of our own destinies adequately explains how I have experienced life so far. Things happen that are unanticipated and yet feel purposeful. It feels like there should be a bigger picture in which this all makes sense, though I am seldom as clear as I would like to be on just what that picture is.

Our church ancestors called this big picture for which I yearn "providence." They would say that what I seek is the plan God has for my life. The Protestant Reformer John Calvin, for instance, described the order and purpose that we sense in the events around us as "the secret stirring of God's hand."[1] Calvin believed nothing happens without God making it happen, from the grand processes of the natural world to the unfolding of human events to the particular experiences in our individual lives. God, Calvin exclaimed, is "the ruler and governor of all things, who in accordance with his wisdom has from the farthest limit of eternity decreed what he was going to do." God makes everything happen, and nothing happens outside of God's wonderful intentions. "Not only heaven and earth and the

1. Calvin, *Institutes*, 210.

inanimate creatures, but also the plans and intentions of [human beings], are so governed by this providence that they are borne by it straight to their appointed end."[2]

When Calvin talks about providence in his writings, he depicts God (more or less) as an actor, making eternal decisions about your life and mine and the events of the world. Once upon a time, I found it helpful to conceive of God as Calvin does, as the grand cosmic actor and agent who sits somewhere beyond the created universe, dictating in specific detail the minutiae of human history and my life. These days, though, Calvin's picture of God is a little too anthropomorphic for me. It relies too heavily on imagining God's providence in basically the same terms as human beings' willfulness—or, shall we say, the way men stereotypically will things: commanding this, that, and the other thing be done, progressing to "their appointed end" by the power of divine decree. That picture of God as a divine lever-puller raises as many questions as it answers, so it does less for me than it once did (certainly less than it did for Calvin, who was responding to the anxieties of his own time and place). Yet this Christian idea of providence—that God is the source of all that is and happens, the One who grants order and meaning to all that is and all that happens—remains attractive to me. It captures a sense of a bigger picture of meaning in which I might make sense of my life, beyond the surprises of luck or the arrogant presumptions of allegedly autonomous choices.

I think theology is more properly understood as poetry than proposition, by which I mean that its function is not to define God but to capture the ineffable experience of God in human words.[3] Good theology does not dissolve into hard categories of true and false. Instead, theology provides evocative language to describe the experience of both the profoundly divine and the mundanely human in life. Theology offers imagistic language for the experiences that resist being captured in empirical assessment, experiences of Something More than material reality. Theology names and honors the mystery in life without reducing it; it deepens our spiritual experiences without necessarily *explaining* them.

The classic Christian language of providence serves that poetic function for me. To talk of providence does not scientifically explain how the pieces of my life come together, but it does invite me to imagine coherent meaning behind those experiences. To talk of providence lyrically reassures me that as I am shaped and reshaped by the circumstances, relationships,

2. Calvin, *Institutes*, 207.

3. My teacher, Doug Ottati, has been especially influential on my thinking on this front. See Ottati, *Hopeful Realism*.

and events in which I find myself, God is present in all of that activity and invested in the impact those experiences have on the person I am becoming. Providence assures me there is more meaning in this world than the sum total of my choices or the accidents (good and bad) that befall me. That meaning resides in "the secret stirrings of God's hand." When we think of providence poetically rather than propositionally, it allows us to put to rest that age-old chicken-and-egg question: How can God control everything and there still be human freedom? As a mathematical formula, true human freedom and absolute divine sovereignty seem to be irresolvable. As poetic imagination, however, providence allows us to see human wills and natural occurrences and the accidents of circumstance as the media through which God communicates investment and meaning in our lives.

There is a school of theology called Personalism, to which Martin Luther King Jr. and others subscribed, that basically argues that personality is the basic element of the universe. That personality, and our individual personalities are what make us unique and valuable people, for personality is also the *imago Dei*, the image of God in each one of us. Personality is the irreducible thing that ties human beings together and to God, among all of the other temporariness in this life. Suspense. I do not think of myself as a Personalist, I like this idea that some inherent aspect of being human ties us to God and makes us more than the sum of our genetic and anatomical parts. In this spirit, the idea of *purpose* functions similarly for me. Purpose, or our desire for meaning, is one of the traits that makes us fundamentally human, and it is something that ties us to the Christian depiction of God. God is Purpose, God has purpose, and that divine purpose is what our Christian ancestors called providence. Providence is the grand connection that weds the events, experiences, and circumstances of our lives together and gives them meaning—and assures us the fingerprints of God are to be found in the tapestry of life these experiences create around us.

Now I am aware this belief in providence brings with it some challenges. The most obvious one is that some unsavory stuff happens in our lives and in the world, and a strong belief in providence would seem to commit "the secret stirrings of God's hand" to that stuff too. A lot of people are put off by a theology that identifies God as the author of the tragedies and traumas of our lives. For many Christians, a theology that insists that God is responsible for everything, including the bad things, threatens our basic conviction that God is good, that God is love.

Past and present, many Christians have felt compelled to answer the question "Why do bad things happen to good people?" with an assertion of God's sovereignty, arguing that yes, the price to pay for confidence in an all-powerful God is that we must admit God green-lights the bad in life too, even if that taxes our understanding of God's goodness. Other Christians have felt compelled to answer this question with an assertion of God's goodness, saying "No, we cannot believe in a God who would predetermine evil to happen without sacrificing the basic Christian confession that God is good." I myself prefer to answer the question with an honest "I don't know." I admit I do not know exactly how to resolve the apparent contradiction between faith in divine providence and faith in divine love. I do not know how to see God as the author of life's great meanings without wondering if that makes God responsible for the meaningless disasters and inhumanities that befall us as well. But I also do not think I need to resolve that tension. I think Christian theology can hold those two claims together. Beyond all else, Christian faith in providential love is God's promise to be with me in all of the bad stuff that happens, and faith in loving providence assures me Paul was right when he promised those Roman Christians long ago that "all things work together for good for those who love God" (Rom 8:28). In some ways, living as a Christian *means* living in the tension between the affirmations of God's providence and God's love.

But trusting in divine providence brings with it another problem: you can't see it. You cannot see the blueprints, so you cannot know for sure you understand the "big picture" of God's intentions, at least not until after the fact. How do you have confidence in something you cannot see, something that often does not make sense? What kind of grand scheme has me raised in blue-collar Appalachia just to end up in collegiate New England? What big picture casts someone as ill-suited in his disposition as me to be the caretaker of children with significant challenges on the path to independence and adulthood? Even if I do believe poetically in a thing called providence, the big picture often eludes me, unless irony *is* the big picture.

In fact, often when I start to perceive a coherent big picture, it turns out not to be the direction my life is going at all. Over the past several years, I have been struggling in my soul with the disconnect between the socioeconomic culture in which I was raised and the institution I now serve. I was raised in rural poverty, and I now work for one of the most class-elite educational institutions in the United States, a college that reinforces and depends on class inequality for its very existence. What in the world is a hillbilly like me doing teaching at a place like Middlebury College? Then a couple of springs ago, a tiny Catholic college twenty minutes from where I grew up advertised for the position of dean of faculty. Well, I thought, this is it. This is the big picture. Raised in that culture, I was given the opportunity to leave western Pennsylvania and experience Middlebury to learn some things—about the liberal arts, about college administration, about the deep problems of access in higher education—so that I could go back and serve "my people." This was the meaning I was looking for. This is what I had been preparing to do for the last dozen and a half years. Providence had shown its secret hand.

Except I did not get the job. What I thought was the obvious end-game that would bring coherence and meaning to all of these incompatible experiences, all the twists and turns, did not happen. To use the language that Christians sometimes use, my plan evidently was not God's plan. To be denied the opportunity to go home when it made so much sense as the big picture (in my reading of the universe, at least) was a crushing blow the likes of which I have not felt in a long time.

Soon after, a good friend who knew about my angst pulled me aside and suggested that perhaps I had the big picture all wrong. Instead of looking to go somewhere that more closely resembles the community that raised me, perhaps I should find a way to make Middlebury College more open and accessible to kids familiar with poverty. At about that time, our vice president of academic affairs announced that she would be stepping down, and I thought, okay, maybe *this* is it. Maybe I have been preparing not to take a little Middlebury to Appalachia, but to bring a little Appalachia to Middlebury. So I threw my hat in the ring to be the next VPAA at Middlebury, eager to make my academic program more hospitable to first-generation students and kids from lower socioeconomic communities.

Except I did not get that position either, which left me with the same questions with which I began, except now just pounding in my head. What in the world am I doing here? Two opportunities, each running in different directions but both offering to help me make sense of the disparate, even contradicting experiences I have had, and neither one of them panned out, despite each in its time seeming to be the obvious answer to my search for ultimate meaning. If there is a big picture to life's experiences, it is frustratingly hard to discern.

But perhaps that is the lesson I am meant to take from a hard season of discernment. I have been looking for a big picture of grand meaning, but perhaps the picture that gives life coherence consists of small and medium-sized sketches that contribute to the larger work. In my case, failures and frustrations over the last several years have refocused me. Maybe the signs of providential intent are not to be found in job ads for college administrators but in the words of a trusted teacher who, in response to musings about administrative work, pulled me aside recently and said somewhat impatiently, "Be a theologian, for crying out loud. You're good at it." Maybe providence's big picture is not to be found in Appalachia but in the students raised in poverty who manage to get to Middlebury and are heartened to find a professor who knows what it took for them to get there. Maybe providence's purpose reveals itself in the personal growth that comes from parenting two delightful kids who often need me to be more than my default. Elijah needed to stop staring into the grand spectacles of earthquakes, wind, and fire in order to hear the voice of providence in the sounds of silence (1 Kgs 19:11–13). Maybe I have been looking in the wrong places for God's plan too.

For it may be that the big picture I have been looking for is not some grand vocational accomplishment for which I have been training my whole life, but instead the work and relationships in the community I now call home—work and people who support me, encourage my growth, give me joy, and instill in life real purpose. If this is the gift I am meant to find, it would seem happily consistent with the God whose loving providence I trust. The signs of providence may be mysterious at first, but God's fingerprints are obvious when we look hard enough for them. Love, care, friendship, and community are the fingerprints of providence; they are the God-given signs of meaning in our lives.

I think I will always look for the secret stirrings of God's hand to make sense of what is around me. It is in my nature. Hopefully I will look with increasing humility to admit that my sense of "the plan" may not be the plan.[4] Whatever the bigger picture is, and despite my uncertainty about it, one thing I know—we all know—for sure. Love, care, friendship, and community are the forensic evidence by which we can say with confidence that "all things work together for good for those who love God." That is the gospel, the hope in which we find purpose. That is the biggest picture of all.

---

4. On the issue of theological humility, Ottati recommends that we "remain agnostic" about the classical assertions of providence. To do so, he says, "does not mean *denying* that God's governance has to do with specific events and/or their arrangement. . . . To remain agnostic about particular and special providence means, instead, that we also recognize that there is much we do not know. It means that, in our own judgment, we do not have sufficient information or warrants at our disposal to make definite claims about specific divine purposes, intentions, whys, and wherefores in very many particular events" (Ottati, *Theology for Liberal Protestants*, 245–46; italics original). This agnosticism is not a reflection of skepticism, but an affirmation of a God-centered piety. "Ruminations about precisely where we fit should, in the end, be tempered by the recognition that we are participants in an enormously longer story of an enormously vast ensemble. But one thing is certain. . . . [The doctrine of providence] encourages us to recognize that God's glory, the image so often proposed as a representation of the *telos* of things by Reformed theologians, is not merely coterminous with human fulfillment; it also intimates genuine incomprehensibility" (254).

2

Beloved Community in the Two Americas

(MLK's Birthday)

I am glad MLK is not around to see this. Faced with the most racially divisive period in the United States since the civil rights movement, many people opine for a Martin Luther King Jr. to remind us of a better vision for the United States of America. But I, for one, am glad Dr. King is not around to see what we have done to his dream. We are not a nation of black, brown, and white children holding hands and playing together, but a country in which people of color remain segregated by real estate, economic opportunity, legal protection, and religious community. We are not a nation in which people are judged by the content of their character; instead, people of color, resident and immigrant, continue to be judged *en masse* as suspicious, radical, ungrateful, violent—in short, a threat. This is not the America of which Dr. King dreamt.

In fact, we are two Americas living in the same national space. One America resembles Dr. King's vision, in aspiration if not in realization. This America recognizes we are becoming increasingly diverse as a nation, with experts projecting people of color will outnumber white citizens in less than a generation.¹ This America welcomes diversity and celebrates how rich and interesting our country becomes with the embrace of racial, ethnic, cultural, and sex/gender difference. This America accepts the truth that to live up to our moniker as the "city on a hill," we must embrace our tradition as a nation of immigrants and establish border policies that are both disciplined and gracious. This America acknowledges that our national history is built on injuries to people of different races, cultures, and countries, but it seeks to remedy that legacy by the confession of sins and commitment to a future of fairness and mutual respect.

The America I have described is one with which millions of us identify, but it is not the only America that exists. There is a second America, gripped by fear and simmering with resentment, inhabited by groups used to occupying the majority and serving as the measure of what is normal, but who now are in danger of losing their country to an element that feels foreign and alien. This is what Robert Jones has called White Christian America, the largely Anglo-Saxon Protestant majority that has controlled American culture and politics for most of our national history.² The citizens of White Christian America sense that their vision of the country is in its death throes. Folks who do not look like them have taken over their neighborhoods, their schools, and their jobs, leaving them feeling unmoored and left behind. People they long considered inferior now occupy important posts in government. Longstanding social norms for authority, family, and religion have been cast aside in the name of diversity. Speech is monitored more closely than ever, with the "political correctness police" now ruling out what would be considered acceptable public vocabulary or pointless banter a decade ago; even jokes are heavily scrutinized for racial undertones and offense to women. The culture is being turned upside down, and if Pat Buchanan was right twenty-five years ago when he declared that there was a culture war being waged in this country, then White Christian America is facing the last great battle for survival, the last opportunity to make America great again. It is Armageddon, with nothing less than the soul of the nation at stake.

For this America, the enemy is "the other," that which is not white or Christian: people of color, immigrants, Muslims, people with strange ways of identifying sex and gender, women with outsized expectations and behavior. In this America, racial bigotry finds a foothold, emboldened by none other than the forty-fifth president of the United States. To White Christian America, this president gives permission to see racist violence in the streets

1. Frey, "U.S. Will Become 'Minority White' in 2045."
2. Jones, *End of White Christian America*.

of Charlottesville as a legitimate difference of opinion between "good people on both sides." To White Christian America, the president recommends a moral distinction between good immigrants from places like Norway and dangerous invaders from "shithole" countries like Mexico, Haiti, and those on the African continent. To thunderous applause from White Christian America, the president dog-whistles four US Congresswomen of color to "go back and help fix the totally broken and crime infested places from which they came," while average citizens follow his lead, badgering Latino residents about their citizenship status or even their use of Spanish in public. This is an America that understands itself to be under siege, and it is lashing out, with presidential approval.

White Christian America harbors white nationalists, of course, but it also is home to a whole lot of other Americans whose views on race are more complicated, who genuinely see themselves as good neighbors and fair-minded people, and yet whose anxieties about the future compel silence or even tepid support when unapologetic racists claim to speak for them. I know this second America, because I lived more than half of my life in it. I grew up in the Rust Belt, in a small coal mining town in southwestern Pennsylvania. I left there to live ten years in the South, where I went to seminary and graduate school. I love those parts of White Christian America. I love the rootedness in community, the sense of place, the intimate relationship with the natural world, the undisputed importance of church. I love the people, who specialize in neighbor-love, who serve as safety nets for one another as second nature, and who know what it means to endure hardship and uncertain futures together. I am happily transported back home again in my mind every time I put on a little Skynyrd, because this part of America is in my DNA.

As a son of White Christian America, I know that not everyone who lives there is a bigot. Living the last twenty years in a college town in northern New England, I bristle constantly at the condescension and judgment leveled at my people in the Rust Belt or Appalachia or the South. I get defensive every time some good-cultured New Englanders listen to an NPR story about "red America" or read *Hillbilly Elegy* and wonder aloud how people can be so backward. My people are not hopelessly ignorant or defiantly racist. My people are good folks who believe in treating individuals with respect, regardless of their skin color; in fact, they often take pride in being "colorblind" this way. Yet, race-baiting and bigotry get traction in this America, abetted by silver-spoon politicians who somehow convince citizens in perpetually depressed economic circumstances that they have their backs.

As a Christian, the greatest tragedy for me is how much of the energy for the defensiveness and besiegement in White Christian America comes from the *Christian* part, specifically the evangelical Protestantism that dominates those areas. Evangelical Christianity has staked its claim in the culture war it wages for our country, and it has anointed its savior, with nearly 80 percent of white evangelicals voting for President Trump in the 2016 election, despite his unconvincing claim to Christian identity and his unapologetically xeno-phobic, racist, sexist, and immoral public and private behavior. In a sense, evangelicalism has made a deal with the devil, concluding that the price of moral integrity was worth the gain of a future for conservative principles like fetal protection and traditional marriage. So evangelicalism baptizes White Christian America and gives its cause righteous power.

But *what shall it profit a man, if he shall gain the whole world, and lose his own soul* (Mark 8:36 KJV)? When Christians give up the moral high ground, purchasing political priorities at the expense of more fundamental ones, how can we ever claim the mantle of moral leadership again? *"You shall love the Lord your God with all your heart, and with all your soul, and with all your mind." This is the first and greatest commandment. And a second is like it: "You shall love your neighbor as yourself." On these two command-ments hang all the law and the prophets* (Matt 22:36–40). How can complic-ity in political divisiveness be a fulfillment of Jesus' great commandments? *When an alien resides with you in your land, you shall not oppress the alien. The alien who resides with you shall be to you as the citizen among you; you shall love the alien as yourself, for you were aliens in the land of Egypt: I am the LORD your God* (Lev 19:33–34). How can the dehumanizing treatment of immigrants be anything but a violation of biblical law? *What does the LORD require of you but to do justice, and to love kindness, and to walk humbly with your God* (Mic 6:8)? How can the racial hatred that runs through the veins of Trump's America be wed to the gospel of Jesus Christ?

Figuring out the best policies to address our immigration problems is a complicated political responsibility, and people of good conscience can disagree over the right balance between border security and the national legacy of welcome symbolized by our Statue of Liberty. Surely, though, we Christians should be united in our denouncement of xenophobic tropes as a strategy for stoking fear in citizens, and the inhuman incarceration of fellow human beings in border concentration camps. Politics is a hard business of deal-making, compromise, and rhetorical persuasion. Politicians bow to the dual masters of serving the nation and getting reelected, and those two mas-ters do not always utter the same commands. Surely, though, we Christians should be of one voice in condemning a politics of name-calling, bald-faced lying, and schoolyard bullying, insisting instead on leadership that binds us together. "What does the LORD require of you but to do justice, and to love kindness, and to walk humbly with your God?" The church should be a force of unity and moral imagination in America, appealing to the better angels of our nation and the best of human moral principle, rather than prostituting itself as a partisan player in an increasingly destructive culture war between the Two Americas.

This unifying moral leadership was, of course, Martin Luther King Jr.'s vision for church in the civil rights movement. He called his fellow Christians to be "creatively maladjusted" for the righteous cause of justice, by which he meant we must refuse to conform to the evils of the world, even if that makes us stand out as troublemakers or radicals. Instead of baptizing injustice or hiding behind the virtue of patience as an excuse to do nothing, we must actively resist the unfairness and hatred that those in power seek to normalize. To exhibit loyalty to the gospel in a culture that subscribes to opposite principles is the great responsibility of Christian witness.

In one famous sermon, King imagined what the apostle Paul would say if he were to write one of his Pastoral Epistles to the American church:

> American Christians, I must say to you what I wrote to the Roman Christians years ago: "Be not conformed to this world: but be ye transformed by the renewing of your mind." You have a dual citizenry. You live both in time and eternity. Your highest loyalty is to God, and not to the mores or the folk-ways, the state or the nation, or any man-made institution . . . In a time when men are surrendering the high values of the faith you must cling to them, and despite the pressures of an alien generation preserve them for children yet unborn. You must be willing to challenge unjust mores, to champion unpopular causes, and to buck the status quo. You are called to be the salt of the earth. You are to be the light of the world. You are to be that vitally active leaven in the lump of the nation.[3]

Faced with a culture of hate that offends the ideals of our faith, Christians must stand with a nonconformity shaped by the gospel of love. Love determines the means and strategies of Christian resistance to this culture, which is why King thought Christian civil disobedience could only be nonviolent. Love also determines our goal, the elimination of cruel inhumanities and the transformation of the culture of hate into an ethos of kinship.

Of course, this emphasis on love is why Dr. King is White Christian America's favorite black preacher, because we have domesticated his message to the point of uselessness. We have remade him into the patron saint of sentimental love, celebrating his vision of brotherhood without any commitment to the justice he understood as the necessary context for kinship.

---

3. King, *Strength to Love*, 138–39.

To talk of love without justice is to distort King's message and to tragically misunderstand the prophetic tradition in which he stood, for the biblical prophets knew there is no love without justice. We cannot love one another when some of us are treated as less than human by a system that benefits the rest of us. King recognized the struggle against institutional racism was not just a matter of the heart but also a matter of law. At their best, just laws are the external form of a society's commitment to love one another as equals. At the very least, just laws are a way to protect the marginalized and vulnerable in a society that is still learning to love as equals.

King assumed reconciliation and peace are impossible unless they are accompanied by true justice. This is a hard message for White Christian America; like the prophet Amos said, "the land is not able to bear all his words" (Amos 7:10). These days it is commonplace for white Americans to agree in broad strokes with the idea of racial harmony, to insist they are not racist because they treat individual people of color with nothing but respect. They bristle, however, when the conversation turns from relationships with individual people to concrete social reforms like affirmative action, financial reparations, or changes to the criminal justice system. These kinds of policies seem to turn the tables, now advantaging people of color, and White Christian America objects to a "reverse racism" that feels no fairer than white bigotry. In the summer of 2019, Senate Majority Leader Mitch McConnell gave voice to White Christian America's normal response when he claimed he did not "think reparations for something that happened 150 years ago, when none of us currently living are responsible, is a good idea." Journalists quickly uncovered that McConnell's ancestors were slaveholders, and he became the poster child for white hypocrisy, given how many white Americans have ancestral ties to slavery.

The moral argument for reparations goes deeper than the culpability of genealogy, however. The idea of reparations is a corrective to the *systemic* legacy of slavery. While slavery ended more than a century and a half ago, its impact reverberates today in the effect racial disparities have on African Americans' legal standing, cultural positioning, and economic opportunity. To call for reparations is not to invoke a punitive penalty on white Americans, and it certainly is not an instance of "reverse racism" (whatever that is).[4] Reparations represent a concrete corrective (even if inevitably

4. Strictly speaking, "racism" is the systemized infusion of racial bigotry into structures of power, in order to reinforce the power of a racially defined majority and oppress racial minority communities. Racism is thus the institutional and systemic marginalization of people along racial lines. Understood this way, it is inaccurate to charge policies meant to mitigate or undo racist systems with being "reverse racism," because these policies (and the marginalized communities they aim to benefit) lack the access to power that racism

insufficient) to an economic system that is skewed significantly against African Americans, a consequence of the aborted intentions of Reconstruction and the subsequent decades of Jim Crow. The same is true of affirmative action policies in housing and education, as well as critiques of the criminal justice system. To insist "black lives matter" does not imply others do not. It is to assert the moral value of a segment of our population that has been systematically oppressed by the society we share.

We white Americans may not be directly responsible for the institution of slavery or its legacy, but we benefit daily from the advantages it provides us, in everything from job interviews to real estate transactions to encounters with law enforcement. In benefiting from that unjust system, we contribute to the myth that it is fair, and that makes us complicit in its injustices. Every white American gets some positive bump from the system by virtue of not being black, even the economically disadvantaged white Americans among whom I was raised. Reparations and other reforms offer a partial correction to a system skewed against people of color, and perhaps a moment of redemption for those of us who profit from its sins.

Reconciliation of the Two Americas cannot be purchased by dispensing with a few racist demagogues or declaring "bygones." It will require real justice in the form of institutional and legal reform. It also will require widespread change in the hearts of White Christian America. Rather than underwriting the sale of America's moral soul to the current occupant of the White House, the church can provide prophetic leadership, bringing America together for the cause of justice. The tentacles of racism are deeply rooted, systemic, and multigenerational—what we Christians call original sin, a violence toward others baked into the fabric of our society. But what John Calvin said about sin is also true of America's racist legacy: it is not our nature but its "corruption."[5] In race relations, as in our other social sins of misogyny and classism, I believe we are more than our worst selves. With God's help and concerted effort, a society in which the residue of slavery still reigns may be transformed one day into the beloved community King imagined, a nation where "justice rolls down like waters, and righteousness like an ever-flowing stream" (Amos 5:24). Until the entire church embraces King's invitation to take up that work, however, this vision for America will remain nothing more than a dream.

---

requires. A critic may or may not consider measures like affirmative action ill-advised, unnecessary, or unfair on other grounds, but they do not constitute something we can call "reverse racism," because they do not serve the end of institutionalizing the power of a racially defined majority. In fact, they aim to disrupt that power.

5. Calvin, *Institutes*, 251.

3

Why God Loves Football

(Super Bowl Sunday)

Each year, on a Sunday in late January or early February, millions of Americans share in a ritual that brings us together as a nation. We congregate all over the US, some of us making arduous pilgrimages to gather before altars appropriate to the occasion. Assembling well before the appointed hour, we engage in various preludes, waiting for the time when we will share food and cup and collectively prostrate before the holiest symbol in our land: the Super Bowl. Super Bowl Sunday is downright religious in the devotion it demands of us. Like Christmas Eve and Easter liturgies, we attend to the Super Bowl in unmatched numbers, even though a healthy proportion of us are not particularly invested in the deeper meanings of the event itself. We attend because that is what you do on this day of the year—and because of the commercials. Despite TV ratings in recent years that suggest the game is not quite the draw it was in its hegemonic height, Super Bowl Sunday remains one of the holiest days of American civil religion.

While some Christians might worry that this cultural ritual smacks of idolatry, I am convinced God is fine with it all because, in fact, God loves football. You will have noticed I offer that last bit as a declaration, not as a question: "Does God love football?" I do not pose it as a question because the question would be entirely rhetorical, for of course God loves football. I am quite certain God loves football, and because I am both an avid student of football and a theologian, you should trust what I say on this matter as true—not just true as a matter of opinion, but true objectively and universally. God loves football. God loves football because football serves as an extended metaphor for what it means to be human. Football refracts for us important dimensions to human experience.

Now, in a moment I will detail some of the ways football shines light on important human experiences that God cares about. But first I want to respond to the question that you may be pondering right now: "Do not all sports serve us this way?" The answer, my friends, is no. God does not love all sports the way God loves football. Some of you are surely tempted to say that baseball is as much a reflection of the divine as football, but you would be tragically wrong. I will admit baseball has a certain elegance and beauty to it that might testify to the creative awesomeness of God. But let's be honest: even God cannot stay awake through a nine-inning Major League Baseball game. I am pretty sure the biblical phrase "weeping and gnashing of teeth" originated as a description of God's reaction to relief pitcher warm-ups. And the baseball playoffs similarly tax God's patience. Several decades ago, it was fashionable to declare that God is dead. I do not believe God is dead, but if God were dead, the cause of death would not be the advent of modern science but the introduction of wild-card teams to the baseball postseason. There is good in baseball, but God clearly does not love it as much as football.

Aficionados of other sports might want to claim a divine endorsement on the level of football, but they would be incorrect as well. Basketball has many virtues, but it also tolerates many false messiahs. Penny Hardaway, Vince Carter, Kobe Bryant, and Lebron James were all hailed as the next Michael Jordan, to predictable disappointment when they turned out to be golden calves. Such idolatry disqualifies basketball as the sport God loves the most. Soccer or hockey? No. For most of those matches, balls and pucks clang around chaotically, like the formlessness and void from which Genesis tells us God created the earth. And then, just when you have stopped paying attention, someone accidentally scores a goal. Soccer and hockey are celebrations of unpredictable luck, and as we followers of the God of Providence know, there is no such thing as luck. So God cannot approve of the message these sports are conveying to our children.

So football it is; God loves football. God loves football because it serves as a prism on human experience, allowing us to see dimensions to being human that are important to being the creatures we are built and called to be. Allow me to suggest just some of the ways in which football edifies us.

First, God loves football because it is beautiful, and beauty is a godly experience. There is an incredible aesthetic appeal to a receiver's well-run route, or the perfect arc on a deep pass, or an exquisitely disguised blitz off the edge. Balls getting to their targets at the right moment, the collision of offensive and defensive players, and the heart-jumping bounce of an increasingly rare onside kick all testify to the grandeur of physics. Football exhibits the beauty in precision and awesome physical power, and the witness to all that beauty and exertion can be a spiritual experience. I am fascinated by the biblical story of Jacob's physical struggle with a stranger on the eve of his reconciliation with Esau (Gen 32:22–32). In his moment of great anxiety and uncertainty, Jacob apparently had an encounter with God in a wrestling match. Similarly, who could witness Odell Beckham's three-finger catch for the New York Giants a couple of years ago and not immediately declare there is a God? The beauty of sports testifies to the wonder of God.

A second reason God loves football is because it serves as an occasion to celebrate family and friendship, in both the playing and watching of it. Friday night high school football games are an important ritual in many local communities' lives, and weekend football games—college and pros— connect many of us with an extended community of fans, some of whom we have never met face to face, but who nonetheless feel like sisters and brothers because of the common love we share. My favorite team, the Pittsburgh Steelers, is a particularly good example of the community-building potential of football. The success of the Steelers in the 1970s—and the 1990s, and the 2000s, mind you—was an occasion for regional pride in a part of the country that otherwise suffers from persistent social and economic depression. The Steelers became a balm to the self-esteem of communities with not much to crow about. And that celebration of identity and heritage continues among Steelers fans, even those who no longer live in the area. If you watch any Steelers away game, you will notice that the number of Steelers fans in attendance rivals the home team's fans. The TV announcers always claim that the Steelers fans "travel well," by which they apparently mean that Steelers fans are underemployed but somehow independently wealthy enough to follow their team across the country. Of course this is not why Steelers fans show up in droves in every other stadium in the NFL. They show up because they already live in those places. In the 1970s, when the Steelers were embarking on a dynasty, southwestern Pennsylvania was in the midst of an economic depression that caused many people to leave in search of work. Those people now live all over the country, but they come together to root for the team that is in their blood. "Steeler Nation" is an exercise in community solidarity, of human fellowship, even among people (like me) who now live in exile from their home. Football can keep us rooted in our communities and our sense of identity; it can connect and reconnect us with people in meaningful ways.

God loves football in that it serves as an instructive metaphor for the best and worst of human beings. At its best, football testifies to the potential in the human will. When we watch that player who becomes a star despite not being drafted, who excels even though scouts declared he lacked strength or speed, who works hard and becomes better than his physical attributes normally should allow, we are reminded that we too are more than the sum total of our physical capabilities. The human potential for accomplishment is not predetermined; heart, grit, and will are our wild cards as well. Football, at its best, also symbolizes our need for community, for a team, for a sense of belonging to feel truly human. Football witnesses to our potential for productive collaboration, as fifty-three players and their coaches work together toward the pursuit of a common goal. Football symbolizes morality and human decency in the formal and informal expectations of sportsmanship that govern the game, at least when it is played well. It highlights human virtues like discipline, focus, effort, and cooperation. In his first letter to the Corinthian Christians, the apostle Paul used running and boxing to illustrate virtues like perseverance and self-control necessary to live the good life in Christ (1 Cor 9:24–27). I am certain that had football been invented in the first century, Paul would have found it an even better metaphor for righteous virtue.

Of course, football also shines light on the less admirable aspects of being human. Football can be excessively rough, even a celebration of violence. The same drive that inspires a player to be the best can also make him narcissistic, as the stereotypical "diva wide receiver" regularly makes plain. A healthy competitive spirit can easily turn into a "win-at-all-costs" consequentialism that justifies actions that the rest of the world—outside of New England, at least—clearly recognizes as cheating. The beautiful game of football is also susceptible to crass capitalism that obscures what is right and good, as both the injustices around student-athlete compensation in college football and the NFL's decades-long foot-dragging around concussions have made all too clear. Yes, there are aspects of football that are not virtuous, that seem to reflect the worst of human nature. Even in those moments, though, we can distinguish between the purity of the game and the sully of human sin. The abuses and perversions of the sport are real and important to acknowledge, but they are not its essence. As John Calvin said about original sin, so we can say about its effect on the righteous game of football: unsportsmanlike conduct is not the nature of football but its degeneration.[1] At its core, football is good.

---

1. Calvin believed in depravity of the human condition, but he rejected the idea that sin was therefore God's fault. In making this argument, Calvin distinguished between the goodness of our original created nature and the corruption of that goodness through our own transgression. See Calvin, *Institutes*, 253.

The excesses of football simply confirm that Aristotle was right: many of the same character traits we celebrate as virtues become flaws if we have too little or too much of them. Aristotle understood virtue to be the practice of the "mean" between character traits that in deficiency or excess were vices.[2] So, for instance, courage is the virtuous mean between cowardice and recklessness, while patience might be seen as the mean between impulsivity and inordinate caution. Too little of such a character trait makes one unwilling to act when a risky situation calls for our help, while too much of the same trait leads us to act too quickly, with insufficient strategy or wisdom. Similarly, football teaches us that the life of virtue is about regulation and discipline, about finding the mean between the excesses of sloth and an unhealthy need to win, a mean we might call healthy competitive effort.

The bad in football also can serve as an effective spotlight on broader cultural sins. Unnecessary roughness symbolizes our penchant for unjustified violence. Players who take advantage of their social privilege in nefarious ways personify the abuse of power that is a tragically systemic social problem. Teams that benefit from their perpetually noncompetitive division to chart an easy path to home-field advantage—while other teams must slug it out in the AFC North—remind us of the hidden advantages of privilege in this country. And sometimes when football casts light on the darker side of humanity, as it has in recent years with the attention paid to domestic abuse among NFL players, it can prompt wider social conversations and action.

Despite, or sometimes because of, its less attractive elements, football ultimately symbolizes the good in human culture, because it displays the complex phenomenon of human creativity, ingenuity, effort, strategy, cooperation, and fun. Each Sunday from pulpits across this country, you can hear preachers demonizing American culture. "The culture tempts us to do X, but Jesus teaches Y," they say. It is true that there is much in American culture that is less than admirable, but culture also reflects human accomplishment, progress, beauty, solidarity, and pleasure. The sinister aspects of human culture are not their nature but their derangement. The enjoyment of football reminds us that there is much in human culture to appreciate and celebrate, that culture is not unambiguously the work of the devil. Culture is part of being human and therefore can be good. I am certain if Jesus lived among us now, he would watch the Super Bowl too. He might even get a chuckle out of the commercials. Football points out to us that there are aspects of culture that are worth appreciating, and for which we should give thanks to the God from whom all good gifts come.

---

2. Aristotle, *Nicomachean Ethics*, 1104a.

Perhaps most importantly, I think God loves football because the game reminds us that having fun is a good and holy thing. Having fun can be an exercise in holiness because in our moments of fun we wring from life the blessings of God. Religion has a reputation—not altogether undeserved—for focusing on the dour and serious. Discipline, duty, and critique are often the hallmarks of religion. We Christians should remind ourselves more often that happiness and fun are part of God's world too, and worthy of religious celebration. I firmly believe grace comes to us not just in serious acts and words of care, but in jokes, levity, recreation, and entertaining distraction. Perhaps there is even a little grace in good-spirited trash-talking; at least I hope so, given how I have disparaged the New England Patriots (and frankly all other sports besides football) in this essay! For me, humor and fun are the truest fingerprints of God upon our lives. When we do not take football too seriously (a warning I do not always heed), it stands for the fun in life, and thinking about football through the lens of our Christian faith can remind us to celebrate fun and recreation and rest, to endorse them with Christian value, and to give thanks to God for the lightness in our lives that assures us of grace.

My confidence that fun is godly derives from my Christian belief in the incarnation. "Christ Jesus . . . though he was in the form of God, did not regard equality with God as something to be exploited, but emptied himself . . . being born in human likeness" (Phil 2:5–7). One basic conviction of our theological tradition is that Jesus Christ is God-with-us, and therefore he represents God's endorsement of human living. The belief that God became human in Jesus is theological affirmation of the human project, in all its embodied, messy fullness. Our time in this life, then, is much more than a temporary assignment from which we hope to be delivered as soon as possible. Christianity has forever fought the temptation to see our creaturely existence as something to regret or reject, when the core of our tradition teaches otherwise. Human living is not only a good gift from God; it is where we encounter God. We encounter God in the struggles and limitations of life, but also in the beauty, wisdom, happiness, and fun of life. That is what it means to believe in God-with-us, Emmanuel, incarnate in Jesus Christ. Life is good. Fun is good. Football is good. And football is just one aspect of human life and culture that can serve as occasion for experiencing the divine.

Not everything that happens in and around the Super Bowl conforms to our religious sensibilities, and we need not excessively baptize this annual ritual of American culture. But I think we Christians can feel free to kick back in front of a game, open up a favorite beverage, gather around friends or family who are dear, and give quiet thanks for football—and for all of the other moments of beauty, connection, rest, and joy that make life worth living, and in which we might catch a glimpse of God-with-us.

4

Friends with Benefits

(Valentine's Day)

I think we all can agree that Christianity and romance have an uncomfortable relationship. Christians talk about love all the time, but we seem better at charitable love than the more intimate kind. We are downright awful about discussing sex, of course, at best fumbling with how to relate the sex life with the life of faith and at worst pitting them against one another. Historically lots of Christian thinkers have regarded sex as antithetical to the life of piety, a distraction from duty and a temptation to sin.[1] When Christians do talk about romantic love, we run straight to marriage, and even our discussions of marriage keep coming back to the same tired tropes. The biblical template of Adam and Eve is a favorite, despite the fact it says nothing explicitly about love or marriage and encourages us to think about

---

1. For much of Christianity's muddled legacy on sex, we have St. Augustine to thank. Next to Jesus and Paul, no thinker has had more of an influence on Western Christianity than Augustine, whose thinking on sex was largely negative and rife with contradiction. Augustine considered sex a natural appetite like hunger, yet he regarded sex acts that are motivated by "lust" (rather than the desire to procreate) to be sinful, even if they occurred within a marital relationship. He considered marriage a good, but he still preferred virginity to marriage as a moral choice. And while he taught that the dutiful fulfillment of a marriage partner's sexual needs was justifiable, he also thought marriage was the "pardon" for a sexual urge that remains sinful on some level, even if it occurs between married people. See Augustine, "Good of Marriage," 71–86.

the relationship between sex and faith as revolving around sin, obligation, child-rearing, and gender differentiation. All of this is to say Valentine's Day may not be Christianity's strong suit.

For a tradition that rotates on the axis of love, then, we Christians stink at talking about romance. One big reason for our struggles with the topic is our religious understanding of love is dominated by one biblical image: the Good Samaritan. For many Christians, Jesus' story of the Samaritan who aids a wounded stranger on the road to Jericho represents the ideal for *agape*, our choice Greek term for love. *Agape*, we are told, is selfless love for the stranger in need. It is "disinterested," by which we mean that we extend it without regard for what we might get in return. It is impartial, meaning that ideally love is not reserved for some people instead of others but is shared with any "neighbor" we encounter who needs an expression of care. And of course, *agape* love manifests in compassionate embraces and helpful actions. It is not about sex at all.

For many people of faith, the Good Samaritan is the sufficient expression of Christian love, of *agape*, and so romantic love would seem to be something else entirely. Worse than this, romantic love might be construed as a threat to *agape*, because romantic love comes with features that are the opposite of what is important about Good Samaritan love. Samaritan love is universal and impartial, extended to neighbor and stranger alike, but romantic love is obviously directed at specific persons and, in our largely monogamous culture, normally to one person at a time. Samaritan love is disinterested and uninvested, extending love as a dutiful response to need, but romantic love is very much interested and invested in the object of affection. Romantic love is mutual, characterized by the giving and receiving of love, in a way that seems more self-serving than Samaritan love. For all of these reasons, many Christian thinkers have regarded romantic love as inferior to the Christian ideal of *agape*, even if romance serves other useful purposes, like the maintenance of domestic partnerships and the propagation of the species.

This perceived antagonism between Christian *agape* and romantic love renders us incapable of saying anything positive about the relationship between sex, romance, and the life of faith. And it is built on a selective grasp of biblical exhortations on love. Jesus told that story of the Good Samaritan to expand our assumptions about who counts as our "neighbor," to widen our sense of duty to perform acts of love and satisfy needs when we are able. Jesus did not mean this to be his only commentary on good Christian love, however, and in fact he provides at least one other description of holy love in the Gospels. In John's account, Jesus describes the love he shared with his disciples as friendship, using the term *agape* to describe this love too.[2] Friendships, as we know, are very specific relationships with other people in which we are invested and mutually connected. Friendships are a much different species of relationship than Good Samaritan stranger-love, yet Jesus insists the kind of intimate relationship he shared with his disciples has holy importance as well. He assures them that friendship may aspire to the ideal of *agape*, the pinnacle of Christian love, when he declares to them: "Greater love has no one than this: to lay down one's life for one's friends" (John 15:13 NIV).

The New Testament Epistles pick up on Jesus' remarks on friendship as an expression of Christian love, and it becomes a primary way for describing the connection between members of the church. Almost all of the epistles were letters written to congregations experiencing conflict, and a consistent theme in these letters is to encourage them to honor the bond they shared with one another as fellow members of the body of Christ, even while they were disagreeing about important theological and moral matters. The First Letter of John is a great example. The main point of that letter is "that we should love one another" (1 John 3:11). Love is our fundamental duty in church because it is our responsibility to reflect the model Christ first gave to us: "We know love by this, that he laid down his life for us— and we ought to lay down our lives for one another" (3:16). The intimate, sacrificial friendship Jesus shared with his first disciples becomes the ethic by which sisters and brothers in the church relate to one another. Good Samaritan stranger-love is good, but so is the more intimate and mutual love practiced within church, the community of friends in Christ.

Similarly, in the First Letter to the Corinthians, right after he assures that disagreeable congregation that the church needs different spiritual gifts and that no gifts are more important than others, Paul reminds them that all of those gifts are meant to be of service to the bond of love that members of the body of Christ ought to share with one another. "If I speak in the tongues of mortals and of angels," he writes in that famous thirteenth chapter, "but do not have love, I am a noisy gong or a clanging cymbal." Paul insists our gifts contribute to church community only insofar as they serve as expressions of our love for other members of the community. Without love between Christians, alleged gifts of the Spirit are empty displays, but infused with the love that endures, they become expressions of *agape* friendship.

Paul suggests in this letter and others that being part of the body of Christ places us in covenantal bond with one another, a relationship of commitment built on our shared allegiance to God in Christ. That bond becomes the context in which we live the life of faith together. In 1 Corinthians

2. For more on friendship as a theological good, see Davis, *Forbearance*, ch. 6.

13, Paul goes on to describe what that love in community ought to look like. Friendship is the partnership in which members of Christ's body practice Christian virtue by extending it to one another. Christian friends show patience, grace, kindness, and humility to others with whom they have differences. We learn how to be good together; we support one another, teach one another, and keep one another accountable. Throughout this passage, Paul uses the term *agape*, but he is not describing the love of a stranger in need here. He is describing the friendship between fellow Christians within a community of faith.

What in the world does all of this have to do with Valentine's Day and the church? Well, I think recovering the importance of friendship to Christian understandings of love gives us a more productive way to think about romantic relationships than all that Good Samaritan talk does. After all, what does it mean to be in a romantic relationship except to be, as the kids say, friends with benefits? Ideally, romantic relationships are a subset of friendship, exclusive and intimate relationships of mutual investment with specific others. Like the broader genus of friendship, a romantic relationship represents a covenantal bond between two persons and a context in which they help one another be better human beings than they are alone. As Jerry Maguire aptly put it, romantic partners complete one another. Romantic relationships ideally serve as opportunities to practice virtue in bonds of mutual support and accountability. We grow as people with the help of those with whom we share our lives in this particularly intimate way.

That is one reason I think the ubiquitous use of 1 Corinthians 13 in weddings (Christian and non-Christian) is appropriate, despite the fact the passage does not actually refer to romantic love. What Paul has to say about Christian friendship here speaks to our theological expectations and hopes for a newly married couple as well. Paul insists when *agape* is the heart of a particular bond, it lives out in the practice of virtue, making us better people in the process. What more could we hope for the particular subspecies of friendship that we bless in a marriage ceremony? Through the honoring of a covenantal commitment with one another under God, two people commit to becoming more virtuous individuals in each other's presence. They pledge deep and abiding friendship to each other, with other benefits too, of course.

Like friendships in general, good romance reminds us we can have exclusive relationships that still leave us open to loving others in different ways. Contrary to what many Christian thinkers have feared, the exclusivity of friendship and romance does no injury to our Christian performance of *agape* in other contexts with other people. I can be a good husband, for instance, without risk to my commitment to the kind of generous stranger-love that the Good Samaritan story commends. In fact, I know I am a more generous soul to others because of the effect of my spouse's love and friendship on my character. When romantic partners deliberately use their relationship to grow in faith and character, they become better equipped to perform Good Samaritan love to others. The practice of romance and friendship can make us better at loving the neighbor and stranger as well.

What difference does it really make, though, to understand romantic relationships theologically through this biblical idea of holy friendship? Quite a lot, I think. The language of friendship gives us Christians something more constructive to say about romance than the stammering, sometimes regrettable utterances of the past. Friendship becomes a basis on which to talk about what really makes for a morally good romantic relationship. It moves us beyond tired debates over acceptable family structures and gender differences to the importance of virtue and accountability in healthy relationships. It reminds us that love, patience, kindness, forbearance, and the commitment to growing in character together represent the ideal for romantic love. In the spirit of 1 Corinthians 13, theologian Margaret Farley insists "the goals of marriage are . . . the goals of love: embodied and inspirited union, companionship, communion, fruitfulness, caring and being cared for, opening to the world of others, and lives made sacred in faithfulness to one another and to God."[3] Is the relationship based on covenantal commitment to mutual respect and accountability? Does it make the partners better people? Is it a working example of 1 Corinthians 13 love? If so, then from a Christian point of view, it would seem to be a godly relationship. Understanding sexual and marital relationships as subsets of friendship helps us focus on what really matters.

The biblical understanding of friendship love also helps us make better sense of those parts of the Bible that have been used too many times as occasions to condemn nontraditional marriages and restrict what counts as holy romance from a Christian point of view. The church is well known for underwriting misogyny and contributing to the oppression of LGBTQIA+ persons, and the Bible is often used as a weapon by Christian combatants in those culture wars. That infamous passage in Ephesians, for instance, where the apostle asks women to "be subject to your husbands as you are to the Lord" (5:21—6:9), has been used to underwrite patriarchy for centuries. Many biblical scholars agree that to read in these verses an endorsement of male authority is to fundamentally misunderstand the passage. Understood in historical context, this passage is more radical than we recognize, for the words challenge the unquestioned and often brutal authority men

3. Farley, *Just Love*, 268.

had over their households in first-century Roman culture. The passage accepts women's duty to obey their husbands, but it goes on to insist that men
be loving to their wives, children, and servants, commending a regard for
other members of the household that was not to be assumed in that time
and place.[4] Families were little kingdoms, not the *Leave It to Beaver* nuclear
bond, making this obligation on men to love their wives as Christ loved
the church more stridently countercultural than it sounds to us today. The
writer of Ephesians was upending, not simply endorsing, gender hierarchies
of his day. The radical intent of Ephesians 5 is made clearer when we read
the passage through the lens of 1 Corinthians 13 and a Christian ethics of
friendship. Then we see more clearly what this passage is trying to do, to
apply the norms of marriage as virtuous friendship to cultural structures of
the time, and in doing so, to righteously challenge those structures.

Understanding sex and marriage through a Christian ethic of friendship also helps us reconcile with another notorious passage from the New
Testament, the first chapter of Paul's Letter to the Romans. To great harm,
verses 26–28 have been cited as evidence that the Bible categorically rejects
homosexuality:

> For this reason God gave them up to degrading passions. Their
> women exchanged natural intercourse for unnatural, and in
> the same way also the men, giving up natural intercourse with
> women, were consumed with passion for one another. Men
> committed shameless acts with men and received in their own
> persons the due penalty for their error. And since they did not
> see fit to acknowledge God, God gave them up to a debased
> mind and to things that should not be done. (Rom 1:26–28)

Here, we are told, Paul is giving us irrefutable evidence that same-sex
relationships are unnatural, immoral, and contrary to Christian teaching.
Again, however, it is unlikely that Paul was talking to the Romans about the
kinds of same-sex relationships that we might have in mind today, committed partnerships between two people who pledge love and fidelity to one
another. Instead, he probably was referring to abusive, exploitative sexual
encounters that were commonplace in Roman culture between men with
power and others (men, women, and children) who were subservient to
them. Those kinds of exploitative sexual encounters transgressed the kind
of virtuous regard for others that Christian faith requires. In other words,
it was the abusiveness of the acts, not the violation of some gender code
for proper relationships, that served as evidence of humanity's sinful ways.
Mark Achtemeier and other biblical scholars urge us to read these apparent

4. See, for instance, Fiorenza, *In Memory of Her*, 266–70.

negative commentaries on homosexuality through the lens of the Bible's constructive theology of sexual and marital love.[5] Measuring them by the rule of 1 Corinthians 13, as I am suggesting we do here, we understand how the fundamental problem being described in Romans 1 is likely not homosexuality but the absence of respectful love and accountability.

Viewing love, sex, and marriage through a Christian ethic of friendship frees us from destructive interpretations of these texts and invites us to evaluate romantic relationships according to the virtues they cultivate and exhibit, not on the forms they take. Understanding romance as a kind of moral friendship allows us to see the good in relationships that do not follow the heterosexual form, and it reminds us that not all heterosexual relationships are good just because they adopt the historically acceptable template. What makes a relationship good and proper, whether between a man and woman or between two people who identify somewhere on the LGBTQIA+ rainbow, is whether it makes the partners better human beings together than they would be alone. Does the relationship encourage the partners to grow in righteous virtue, to love each other and their neighbors with kindness, patience, humility, and generosity? When two people commit to one another and to God in a covenantal relationship, to support one another, to grow with and into one another, to be accountable to each other, then it is good. The moral friendship described in 1 Corinthians 13 provides theological rationale for us to embrace what the culture around us seems to have realized much faster than the church, that there may be holiness and profundity in romantic relationships that resemble something other than Adam and Eve.

Margaret Farley assures us "love is true and just, right and good, insofar as it is a true response to the reality of the beloved, a genuine union between the one who loves and the one loved, and an accurate and adequate affective affirmation of the beloved."[6] That is a mouthful to put on a valentine, but it is a wise and mature assessment of true love from a theological perspective. Good love enables us to love the other, to see the other as a person with hopes, needs, and integrity, and not just as a satisfaction of our desires or an extension of our self-concern. This kind of love between partners in turn makes those partners better lovers of people beyond their romantic relationship. True love makes us better human beings than we are alone. Regardless of the particular form it takes, romantic love is good when it cultivates mutuality, justice, respect, and virtue in the lives of those who enjoy it. At its moral heart, good romance is good friendship—with other benefits, of course.

5 Achtemeier, *Bible's Yes to Same-Sex Marriage*.

6. Farley, *Just Love*, 198.

5

Not in the Eyes of the Beholder

(First Day of Spring)

In Vermont, we are fond of referring to spring as "mud season." As the landscape emerges from its snow-covered hibernation, the ground struggles to find room for all the water produced by the melting snow. So the water sits on top, creating mud everywhere that seems to last for weeks. Every responsible homeowner possesses planks or plywood up to the task of serving as a makeshift bridge, essential for getting from driveway to aptly named mudrooms in the house. Otherwise-routine trips into town now require a check of local traffic news to ensure roads and bridges have not been overtaken by the water and mud looking for somewhere to go. Yesterday's farm field is a lake today, complete with ducks and geese taking advantage of the flash body of water. And most of the cars on the roads in March and April look like they have been off-roading. Last spring I discovered what a horrible mistake I had made when I traded in my old tan pickup truck for a shiny new black one.

We complain a lot about mud season here, but truth be told, there is more to spring in Vermont than mud. Nature awakens from its long winter nap with bright skies and crisp breezes that convey hope and promise renewal. The same melt-off that creates all the mud also fills Vermont's many streams, brooks, and creeks to capacity (or beyond), and the water crashing down the falls of Otter Creek offers a stunning display of power and beauty. Wildlife makes appearances where the scene was desolate and lonely only weeks ago, and the college students I teach seem happy again too, released (at least for a bit) from the pressure of exams and papers by the enticement of a Frisbee game on the campus lawn. The warmth of the sun is beautiful. The emergent grass is beautiful. Heck, even the mud is a beautiful sight to bear, after months of frigid cold and fleeting daylight. Like every other season of the year, spring in Vermont reminds us of what beauty looks like, at least for those of us fortunate enough to experience it.

Celebrating beauty in the natural world is not just a preoccupation for flannel-wearing, granola-crunching Vermonters. It strikes me as a foundational Christian celebration too, because it is how the Bible starts telling the story of God's love affair with the world. Contrary to popular belief on both sides of the tired conservative-liberal debate, the biblical creation story was never meant to be a roadmap or recipe for how the universe was actually created. Our ancient ancestors were more imaginative with language than we sometimes are. They were not saddled with the modern conflation of "data" with "truth." The opening lines of Genesis offer not an "explanation" of creation, but a poetic celebration of it. They declare a confession of faith that God is the animating force behind the universe in which we reside. They celebrate the inherent value in the cosmos. The world around and beyond us humans is good. We know this because Genesis not so subtly tells us in stanza after stanza of this creation ode that "God saw that it was good"—until the end of the creative process, when God gazes on a mature natural order at the apex of a celebratory crescendo: "God saw everything that [God] had made, and indeed, it was very good" (Gen 1:31).

But why was it good? If we insist on viewing everything as if human beings are the center of the universe, then we might be tempted to think creation was good because it was set up perfectly to serve us human beings. It was good because it was good *for us*. There is no denying that Christians in the West historically have interpreted Genesis exactly this way. We in the West declared long ago that creation was designed for our good use. We focused on that mandate to "have dominion" over creation (v. 28), and we took it as license to control creation, to use it, to consume it for our own purposes and expansion upon the earth.[1] These days our consumption

---

1. In 1967, historian Lynn White Jr. wrote an essay titled "The Historical Roots of Our Ecologic Crisis," in which he charged Western Christianity with providing the ideological justification for human devastation of the environment. According to White, Christianity's emphasis on God's biblical mandate to "subdue" and "have dominion" over creation gave modern industrializing capitalist societies in the West theological permission to view the natural world solely as a resource for human consumption. This

mentality conspires with the triumph of the market in contemporary culture to define the natural world as "good" only insofar as it feeds us, clothes us, and runs our cars, leading us to the obvious judgment that the natural world has instrumental value only. It is good because it is good for us. It is valuable as a resource for our consumption.

There is no denying that the Bible has helped Christians draw that conclusion. God instructs the first human beings in Genesis to "be fruitful and multiply, and fill the earth and subdue it, and have dominion" over it. But there is also no denying that the ancient writers who gave us those words could not possibly have imagined a modern society that would literally subdue nature, bringing it to its knees. To the contrary, nature always had the upper hand to the ancients. It was more powerful, wild, mysterious, and dangerous. The challenge to fill the earth and subdue it was likely nothing more than a divine pep talk, to see the world as a good rather than a source of fear. The invitation to subdue was encouragement in a time when nature seemed downright scary; I doubt that these lines were penned with the idea of dominating the creation into extinction.

At any rate, the lines about dominion do not tell us *why* God considers the creation good, despite our historic assumptions that they do. The Genesis creation story does not say God declared creation good because it was perfect for the voracious appetites of the human species. The Genesis creation story simply says God looked upon all that God had made, including human community, and declared it all very good—good because it *was*, good in its being. And it was so good in itself that God took a whole other day to relish the beauty of the universe, a day called Sabbath, a habit commended to us as well.

So maybe the world is not good because of its usefulness, but just because it is *beautiful*. It is beautiful not because we say it is, but because God declares it is. Its beauty flows from God's own animating beauty. Recently I revisited one of my favorite thinkers, the eighteenth-century American theologian Jonathan Edwards. Now to the extent they know Edwards at all, most people know him as the author of that stereotypical Calvinist sermon, "Sinners in the Hands of an Angry God," so they imagine Edwards as a fiery revivalist preacher, hammering damnation and whipping up spiritual

---

essay is widely taught in environmental studies programs across the country, and it has been enormously influential in popularizing the argument that Western Christendom is predominantly responsible for our current environmental crisis. Unfortunately, the voices in the Christian tradition that have focused on love and respect for the natural world (and that animate current Christian environmentalism) get less attention, even though White himself acknowledged St. Francis of Assisi as one Christian perspective that exhibits more care for and solidarity with the nonhuman world than the "dominion" attitude he highlighted.

anxiety. Actually that sermon is atypical of his writing, certainly not indicative enough to deserve the exclusive attention it gets. In reality, Edwards was one of the sharpest theological and philosophical thinkers in American history, and his larger works fuse Calvinist theology with the Enlightenment that was also profoundly influential on him in his time. He read John Calvin and the Puritans who preceded him, but he also read John Locke and Francis Hutcheson and learned from David Hume, stalwarts of early modern philosophy. To my mind, that fusion remains a compelling read today.

Edwards wrote an interesting treatise called *The Nature of True Virtue*, in which he claims that true virtue is a subset of a larger reality he calls beauty. Beauty as we normally experience it in life is the apprehension of things in "mutual agreement," a "visible fitness of a thing to its use" that is pleasing to us, rationally and emotionally.[2] It is the experience of things like order, proportionality, and agreement, or the delight we feel when something fits smartly as part of a greater impressive whole. Edwards believed that this beauty we experience in the world around us reflects "some image of the true, spiritual original beauty," which he understood as "union and consent with the great whole" of Being in general (that is, God).[3] In other words, experiences of natural, aesthetic, or proportional beauty are secondary reflections of God's beauty, and they participate to some degree in the beauty of the divine. I understand Edwards to be saying that we experience things as beautiful—physically, emotionally beautiful, or morally beautiful—when we are struck by the way they reflect the goodness of God and the wonder of God's "big picture" in which we all exist.

Edwards is adamant that things are not beautiful because we say they are. Our experiences or preferences are not what makes something beautiful. We sense beauty in our world because those things are beautiful already, and they are beautiful because they participate in God. God is "the ground both of their existence and their beauty."[4] The beauty we encounter in this world emanates from God's beauty and participates in it. God is the source of the beauty we experience, and the experience of beauty in our world is the experience of God. So despite the popularity of the cliché, it turns out that beauty is *not* in the eyes of the beholder, at least not if the beholder is mortal. Beauty resides in the heart of God and extends outward to the things we experience as beautiful, and in that way beauty is a reflection of the *inherent* value of the things we behold. Beauty is a gift, to the one who is beautiful and the one who regards that beauty.

2. Edwards, *Nature of True Virtue*, 561–63.
3. Edwards, *Nature of True Virtue*, 550, 564.
4. Edwards, *Nature of True Virtue*, 542.

To experience beauty in the world is to participate in the divine. Listening to wind rushing through tall pines on an otherwise silent walk can be an encounter with God. Taking in the intensity of green on a countryside in June can be a spiritual epiphany. Gazing with wonder on the intricate camouflage worn by the tree frogs who have moved in on my front porch is an experience of the holy. Sitting back to admire the orderliness of a mathematical proof or to ponder the precision of a logical argument can be soul food, for these are all beautiful. Basking in the serenity of a simple afternoon, following your lovely spouse in tow as she makes her way around a local nursery, is beautiful. Sharing friendship in a loving community is beautiful, for love is also something that we call beautiful. All of these experiences of beauty are participation in the divine.

John Calvin believed something similar. Taking St. Augustine's ancient definition of the sacraments—"visible signs of an invisible grace"—he argued that, generally speaking, a whole lot of our experiences are tangible indicators of God's loving care and intimate presence.[5] A lot of things in our lives strike us as profound signs of God's invisible grace. Broadly speaking, we have more opportunities for sacramental experience than just our baptism and sharing the Lord's Supper; nature can offer sacramental experiences, and Calvin's favorite example was the rainbow.[6] A rainbow, he argued, in its inherent beauty and surprising rarity, in its ancient symbolism of the benevolent promises of God, is a visible sign of God's invisible grace. Gazing on a rainbow can be a sacramental experience, an invitation to commune with God.

The world in which we live and the people with whom we share it are beautiful not because we experience them that way or declare them to be. By extension, nothing in the world or among its people is ugly or unattractive because some of us declare it so. The world and its inhabitants are beautiful because we participate together in the beauty that first emanates from God. The God who is Beauty declares us and our world "very good." That goes for ourselves too, by the way. In a culture that insists on defining beauty by Hollywood standards, and where young people and the aging alike struggle to see themselves in that definition, we are reminded that these claims to beauty are false gods. To be beautiful does not demand that we be leggy, cut, or wrinkle-free. God gives us our beauty, which is there whether people recognize it or not. It is inherent value, inherent goodness, inherent worth and blessing.

5. Calvin, *Institutes*, 1277.
6. Calvin, *Institutes*, 1294.

As with everything else in the Christian life, the gift of beauty comes with corresponding responsibility. Ecologically, we have a righteous responsibility to preserve and protect that which God has given us as beautiful, to do what we can to sustain the beauty in this wonderful world God has given us, not just so there will be an earth for future generations of people to use, but because it is God's world and valuable *as such*. We have a righteous responsibility to protect it, but just as importantly, we have a delightful obligation to enjoy the world and give thanks for it.

Interpersonally, we have a responsibility to name the beauty in ourselves and others, especially to drown out the voices that define beauty in restricted ways. Especially to the bullied and harrassed, to the marginalized and ostracized, to those who do not conform to what society considers right or normal, we are charged as the ambassadors of God to declare the truth: you are beautiful, just as you are, because God loves you as you are.

There is a lot of mud in the world right now. It is mud season in our politics, media, entertainment, schools, and communities—not just on the ground in the Green Mountain State. Maybe what the world needs right now is people who point out the beauty in the midst of the mud, who remind us the experience of the world and our engagement with one another can be sacramentally blissful, as we see in the world and one another the visible signs of God's invisible grace. Calling out beauty when we see it, everywhere, sounds like a suitable job for the people called church.

6

In Our Joy Disbelieving

(Easter Day)

I was having breakfast with a faculty colleague this week, and the subject of church came up. My friend grew up in the Roman Catholic Church, but he does not associate with his religion anymore. "Someday you and I need to have a conversation about this church thing," he said to me. "I have to admit that I have distanced myself from that stuff in my middle age. I guess I am too much of a scientist; I need things to be empirically validated to believe them. I would love to talk to you about how you keep religion and the life of the mind together." Many of us have had similar conversations; some of us have them with ourselves. We are not always sure we buy the things read and claimed at church. What do we do with the disconnect between the assertions of the faith and the requirements of the critical mind?

Exhibit A for the unreasonableness of Christianity is usually the prevalence of miracles in our sacred texts. Convention suggests that what makes a miracle a miracle is its magical quality, something that is otherwise inexplicable, that bends the logic of time, space, or causality. That is literally the definition of a miracle: "a surprising and welcome event that is not explicable by natural or scientific laws and is therefore considered to be the work of a divine agency." (I know, because as a serious academic, I googled it.) There are plenty of accounts in Scripture that follow this definition, and there are plenty of people today who believe in these kinds of miracles and wait on them in their lives. But if you struggle with the idea that God regularly works by suspending the laws of nature, then these miraculous stories may become less compelling to you. You may be tempted to ignore or dismiss them because they seem so fantastical, because they run counter to the way we understand the world to work. No less a thinker than Thomas Jefferson famously rejected the biblical miracle stories for just this reason, literally cutting them out of his Bible. And if we find the stories themselves unbelievable, then we may not be persuaded that the point they are trying to make with tales of wonder is compelling either.

Easter is the Christian season that brings this question of the reasonableness of faith most acutely to mind. After all, this is the season of resurrection, one of the most fantastic claims of Christian faith. God raised Jesus from the dead. Historically the entire Christian confession rests on that claim. The resurrection is the vindication of Jesus' life and the symbol of God's victory over sin and death. The resurrection is the foundation on which Christian hope is built. Historically Christians have witnessed to the resurrection as the indicator that Jesus is the Son of God and that God's promise of triumph over sin and death is trustworthy. Without the resurrection, Jesus is Mahatma Gandhi or Martin Luther King Jr., but probably nothing more.

But the idea of resurrection—physically coming back from the dead—taxes the modern mind. It seems fantastical, an obvious violation of things we take for granted about the normal order of being alive and being dead. How do we navigate that seeming disconnect between faith and reason?

Perhaps we could start by affirming just how righteous the experience of doubt, confusion, and uncertainty is, particularly around this notion of resurrection. Doubt and confusion appear to be common biblical responses to the proclamation that God raised Jesus from the dead. In the Gospels, the confrontation with a risen Jesus arouses disbelief and wonder in his disciples. Luke puts it this way: "While in their joy they were disbelieving and still wondering . . ." (Luke 24:41). That is one of my favorite phrases in all of Scripture! Luke does not describe their response to the encounter with Jesus as a simple epiphany, as in "Oh, we thought you were dead, but now we see you are clearly alive, and now we get it. Yay!" No, Luke describes those disciples, who have bumbled their way through the journey with Jesus to the cross, as still fumbling with this experience. And the tense of the verbs Luke uses is telling. The disciples "were disbelieving" and "still wondering," experiencing doubt and confusion that continued into the future. They were not getting past their wondering and disbelieving quickly, but rather than a source of distress, they experienced it as part of the joy of an encounter with Christ.

Doubt and uncertainty are portrayed here not as impediments to intimacy with Christ but as components of the experience. Neither does the uncertainty go away, for it continues into the writing of the Gospels themselves, each of which has a different take on the ending of Jesus' story. Together they are confused about what to make of the experience of the risen Jesus, suggesting the early church was still uncertain as to how to talk about the resurrection years after the experience of the first disciples.

The author of the Gospel of Mark evidently was so uncertain that he originally said nothing at all about Jesus' post-resurrection appearance, ending his Gospel with a secondhand account of the empty grave. An angel pronounced Jesus risen, and the women who visited the grave "went out and fled from the tomb, for terror and amazement had seized them, and they said nothing to anyone, for they were afraid" (Mark 16:8). The End. The Gospel ends with a claim of resurrection and a fearful and bewildered response. That is it. Only generations later did somebody find that ending unsatisfying and add something else, followed by another editor who tried a second attempt to fill the gap. The Gospel of Mark appears in our Bible with what scholars recognize as three separate endings, the original and then two subsequent interpretations and embellishments of a piece of good news that was hard to fathom.

The other Gospels reflect confusion about the resurrection in their own ways. Matthew portrays Jesus physically present enough that some of the disciples could grab his ankles, and yet he flits in and out of situations like a ghost. Matthew also tells us that when encountered with the risen Jesus, the disciples "worshiped him, but some doubted" (Matt 28:17). The Gospel of John depicts Jesus as appearing in the presence of the disciples with the physical scars of crucifixion, but also walking through locked doors (John 20:19–20). Luke describes Jesus suddenly appearing in the disciples' midst, as if out of thin air, and then asking for lunch (Luke 24:41–43). The Gospel writers clearly were unsure how to account for the confession that Jesus has been raised from the dead.

Likewise, many people still do not know exactly what to make of these claims of resurrection. Was Jesus physically, bodily present with the disciples in a life after death, in a way that defies what we know to be scientifically possible? Was Jesus spiritually present with those early followers, in a way that made a lasting impression on the Christian community, and which they described as "bodily resurrection" in order to capture the powerful impact of the spiritual encounter? Which of these explanations is more faithful?

Which should we believe to be true? Or is there another compelling explanation altogether?

Asking these kinds of questions about something as important as the resurrection may feel like a crisis of faith, but I do not think it needs to be. What we see from the Gospel narratives is that uncertainty is a natural component of faith, not an injury to it. Part of our problem in dealing with our doubts and questions is that in the modern era we have changed what "faith" means. These days many Christians assume that having faith requires accepting certain biblical claims as literally true. If you have faith in the power of God, then you need to believe miracles happen in exactly the science-defying way the Bible describes them. If you have faith in the resurrected Christ, you need to accept that Jesus was raised from the dead, literally, exactly as the Bible describes it. If you question the bodily resurrection of Jesus, you are saying it is not true, which means you lack faith.

As we have seen, though, that makes qualifying for faithfulness a difficult assignment, because the Bible describes miracles and resurrection in less certain ways than the insistence on certitude can accommodate. Just as importantly, assent to propositional claims is historically not what faith meant in Christian circles, at least not until the twentieth century. About a hundred years ago, some Christians began to worry about the effect of modern science and knowledge on traditional religious convictions. Scientific explanations of the natural order seemed to contradict the Bible's creation stories. Modern astronomy raised questions about biblical accounts of the sun standing still and stars pointing the way to the Messiah. Archaeology and textual study were even changing the way people read the Bible, disclosing to us stories behind these ancient texts and ushering in what is now called the historical-critical methods of biblical interpretation. Worried Christians saw intellectual innovation as a threat to faith, and in response they doubled down on what they considered the "fundamentals" of Christianity. They made a list of them—things like belief in the inerrancy of Scripture, the virgin birth, and the bodily resurrection of Christ—and insisted that true faith required Christians to subscribe to these tenets. They were the first fundamentalists, and their struggle against science reached an early apex in the title fight over evolution in the Scopes trial of 1925.

Unsurprisingly, this assumption that faith means propositional assent also has been accepted as gospel by modern rationalists, skeptics, and other "cultured despisers" of Christianity. They too assume that to be a person of faith means you must accept as true fantastical claims derived from a literal reading of the Bible. Faith, then, is antithetical to reason, because to be counted as a rational and modern person you must reject the idea of bodily resurrection, miracles, and indeed the unprovable existence of God as patently untrue. The so-called New Atheists several years ago made a name for themselves—and sold a lot of books—on the premise that faith requires anti-intellectual assent to the literal believability of biblical stories. Richard Dawkins declared all people of faith "delusional" because the claim to faith itself required setting aside intellectual integrity, while TV personality Bill Maher continues to amuse himself by regularly declaring all religious people to be ridiculous.[1]

For the fundamentalist and the skeptic, the essential measure of faith seems to be this: Do you believe the events in the Bible actually happened the way they are depicted? That is what we have done to faith in the modern era. But over the long trajectory of Christian believing, that is not what faith meant at all. Faith was not assent to propositional factual claims but trust in the promises of God, and the biblical and theological traditions were the poetic expressions of God's promises as they were experienced in communities of faith.[2]

Some might hear this suggestion—that faith does not require that we take the Bible at its literal word—as another liberal challenge to Scripture's authority. To take the miracle stories at something other than face value is to say they are not true, or that God cannot do what the Bible says God can do. But to read the miracle stories or accounts of resurrection in a way other than as play-by-play of actual events does not need to imply a challenge to biblical authority or the power of God. Quite the contrary, to read these stories as having meaning beyond the magical is to reaffirm the enduring wisdom and authority of the Bible in our time, to insist God acts even by means we think have other explanations. Understood this way, I think some of these stories testify *more* powerfully to the glory and providential care of God, because they do not require us to temporarily suspend our understanding of the way God's complicated world works in order to affirm that God is good, that God is at work in the world, and that God provides.

For example, generations of biblical scholars have wrestled with the story of manna from heaven coming to the Israelites while they wandered

1. Dawkins, *God Delusion*. Dawkins is perhaps the most commercially successful of the New Atheists, a group of public intellectuals who made a name for themselves attacking the alleged irrationality of religion. Although he does not contribute academic arguments to the cause, Bill Maher has long parroted the New Atheists for his television crowds.

2. Davis, *Forbearance*, 90–98. Michael Langford points out that this connotation of faith as trust or "willingness to live in accordance with the beliefs one has come to hold" is a more faithful rendering of the New Testament word usually translated as "faith," *pistis*. Langford agrees that if faith means "trust" or "commitment" more than "irrevocable belief," then "the opposite of faith is not doubt but faithlessness, or the lack of serious commitment." See Langford, *Tradition of Liberal Theology*, 11.

in the wilderness. No one knows for sure what that manna was. Heck, the Israelites didn't know! The word *manna* itself means "what in the world is this?" Because it was not clearly identified in the text, modern biblical scholars have come up with all kinds of possible explanations. Was "bread from heaven" the sap from a tree that the Israelites were unfamiliar with? Or was it a heretofore unknown fungus? Was it the protein-rich secretion of a desert insect? We Christians can react to these efforts at explanation a couple different ways. We may suspect they are dismissals of the miraculous power of God, but we also may understand them as *reaffirmation* of the loving providence of God, because they testify to the wonderful ways God works through secondary causes in God's complex universe, through the mundane as well as the apparently inexplicable. In some ways, seeing God's providence in what we can explain scientifically is a greater exercise of faith than looking for God in the fantastical. Recognizing God providing through the secretions of a bug no one knew existed out in the desert, or some other acknowledgment of God's miraculous abundance in a detail of the everyday, takes more seasoned eyes of faith than assuming God only works through an obvious show of power.

Similarly, faith in the resurrection need not rest on a single explanation of exactly what happened. If it did, which Gospel account would you pick? Faith in the resurrection means trusting in the promises of God that are packed in that evocative proclamation that God raised Jesus from the dead. What are those promises? Well, here are a few. That God is persistent love. That God's love will pursue us to and beyond the grave. That God's love is more powerful than human destructiveness. That God's love is more powerful than death. That through the spirit of Christ, God's love endures with us, through time and space. That the way of Jesus is a faithful testament to what God's love looks like in the project of human living. That the way of Jesus is the path to experiencing authentic life in loving community, as we are meant to live. That this kind of love and grace are the moral axes on which the cosmos revolves, no matter what the forces around us suggest to the contrary. That is *at least* what faith in the risen Jesus means.

Intellectual and theological humility reminds us that to claim rock-solid confidence in one interpretation of the resurrection is to claim more than the Gospels themselves are willing to assert. (Not for nothing, fellow liberals, humility also cautions us against excessive confidence in our ability to know what did *not* happen.) If faith in the resurrection is not unwavering subscription to a concrete account of biblical events, though, what does it mean to gather as the Easter people? What does it mean to be the body of the risen Christ, and to invite others to join us in that identity as well? What does it mean to gather and proclaim with Christians of every time and place that God raised Jesus from the dead?

To me it means to gather together in the promises of God, in hope and faith that (as the apostle Paul puts it) "neither death, nor life, nor angels, nor rulers, nor things present, nor things to come, nor powers, nor height, nor depth, nor anything else in all creation, will be able to separate us from the love of God in Christ Jesus our Lord" (Rom 8:38–39). It means to gather with confidence in God's love, enough that we might call ourselves "children of God" (1 John 3:1), a community dedicated to living the Way of Jesus, proclaiming the love of Jesus, and inviting others to experience renewed life on this pilgrimage with us. To gather as Easter people means to commit to studying our heritage as Jesus did with those disciples he met up with on the road to Emmaus, mining old words for fresh truths, wisdom from the past to inspire wisdom for today (Luke 24:13–35). It means to consider *and reconsider* what we believe to be good and true—to walk together in a process of discovery and doubting, of asking questions and sitting with answers—and to do so in the dual promise that God will not abandon us for our questioning, and neither will an authentically Christian community of faith.

Easter people can expect to have moments of disbelieving and wondering in their joyous life together, and they can expect in their disbelieving and wondering to find joy! To be Easter people means to live together in the loving grace of God embodied in the continuing presence of Jesus with us, to practice Christ-like grace with one another through our seasons of confidence and our periods of uncertainty, and to invite others to do the same. I think that is what it means to be the body of the risen Christ in this modern, scientific, rational, skeptical, self-interested, impatient, divisive, demythologized world in which we live. We gather in this resurrection theology: God is good, grace is enduring, and mystery and uncertainty are part of the journey. Through all the confusion, doubt, and wondering, we remain steadfast in one truth: that nothing will separate us from the love of God, or from each other, in Christ Jesus our risen Lord.

7

Mothering as Resistance

(Mother's Day)

In 2018, Tammy Duckworth made history, becoming the first US senator ever to cast a vote on the Senate floor with a baby in her arms. It took some doing; the Senate first had to change a longstanding rule that prohibited babies on the floor of the Senate, and changing Senate rules does not happen easily. (Apparently, the last time the Senate had changed the rules for who or what had floor privileges was in 1977, when they voted to allow service dogs.) Duckworth and others worked for months to change the rule, answering questions like whether this would mean diapers could be changed on the Senate floor, or whether the baby would have to adhere to the Senate dress code. Ultimately, though, the rule was changed to allow senators to bring their newborns onto the Senate floor and even to breast-feed them if needed. And so Tammy Duckworth, US senator and new mom, cast a vote with her child right there with her.

Of course, the news media covered the event with enthusiasm for its rarity. It was rare largely because of the limited number of women who have exercised privileges on the floor of the United States Senate. In the history of the body, only fifty-two women have been members—twenty-three of them serve today, an all-time high. So the sight of Senator Duckworth bringing her baby into the Senate was a symbol of the way tradition has been forced to evolve under the pressures of gender equity. But beyond the celebration of justice and progress, I was struck by the power in the juxtaposition—one individual holding together in a single moment four distinct identities: woman, military veteran, political leader, mother. And the infiltration of mothering, with all of the connotations it brings—nurture, protection, love, sacrifice—into a body regarded by many Americans as mired in futility, impotence, and destructiveness, spoke a word of prophetic resistance in that moment to politics as usual. Insisting on bringing her young child to the halls of government, Duckworth did more than demand workplace accommodations. She offered a display of mothering as an act of resistance to disordered power.

Celebrating Mother's Day in the church, frankly, is wrought with opportunities to do something dumb. And to be honest, churches often avail themselves of those opportunities. I spent a decade in the South, where Mother's Day is a national holiday of almost unrivaled proportion. During my time in Virginia, I was part of at least one congregation that insisted on handing out roses to all the "moms and potential moms"—which meant all of the women in the congregation. The problems with that practice are legion, of course. It collapses womanhood into motherhood, thus conveying the message that what is most essential about being a woman is becoming a mother, implying that the other things women might do—like giving your legs in service to the US military or becoming a US Senator, both things that Tammy Duckworth did—are distractions from a woman's real reason for being. The sentimentalizing of motherhood ignores the possibility that many women choose not to have families, and it runs roughshod over the reality that many women who want to experience childbirth cannot. It aggravates the pain that many people associate with motherhood—the loss of children, the loss of beloved mothers, the estrangement from mothers with whom we might have difficult and disappointing relationships.

But another problem with the sentimental celebration of Mother's Day in the church is the way we domesticate motherhood. As pushback on that domestication, Senator Duckworth's story reminds us that mothering also can be an intense and important political act, a public display of priorities and virtues that are the best of who we are as human beings, and that stand in judgment against the worst of our inhumanities.

Of course the Bible offers several subversive stories of women doing the same, resisting unjust political power through the role of mother. One of my favorites is the story of Moses' birth mother in the book of Exodus (2:1–10). It is easy to read the story of Moses' mother in other ways: as the personal tragedy of a woman forced to yield her child, as an illustration of the moral ambiguities in adoption, or as a testament to God's sovereignty.

But it seems clear to me that Exodus offers us this story as an essential part of a tale of political resistance. We are told the Hebrew people, who found refuge in Egypt during periods of famine, had grown strong in number over time. The Egyptian pharaoh feared these immigrants in his land would crowd out, overwhelm, and threaten his good native people. Finding it too late to build a wall, he conspired instead to kill the baby boys born of the Hebrews. He tasked the midwives of the land with this murderous chore, but the women resisted, refusing to be complicit in pharaoh's schemes, instead deceiving him to spare the children.

Scripture tells us one Hebrew woman resisted the political powers of evil and death in a particularly painful but potent way. She gave birth to a son, and in order to spare his life, she concocted a plan to have him "discovered" by the pharaoh's own daughter. Pharaoh's daughter did discover him and claimed him as her own, thereby saving his life. And when pharaoh's daughter then needed someone to feed and care for him, Moses' mother positioned herself to get him back. An artful and courageous act of care to ensure her child would live.

But is that all it was? We know Moses grew up to become the liberator of the Hebrew people, and it strikes me that Exodus tells this story as more than a sentimental tale of maternal sacrifice. In the story of the Hebrew people's liberation from Egypt, Moses' mother commits the first act of political resistance. In preserving the life of her child, aggressively and with righteous guile, she thwarts a homicidal regime, fulfills her duty to her people, and makes herself available as an instrument of God's justice. Hers is a story of mothering as an act of political resistance.

For Christians, the most important example of the political significance of mothering is Mary, the mother of Jesus. We rarely think of Mary in political terms. For generations, Mary has been depicted as the meek and mild "handmaiden of the Lord," whose chief virtue was acquiescence to God's salvific plan. But a different Mary emerges from a careful reading of the song she sings in the Gospel of Luke, in response to the announcement that she will carry the Messiah of God (Luke 1:46–55). Echoing the prayer of Hannah, the mother of Israel's great prophet Samuel, Mary "magnifies the Lord" for the good news that she will birth the Savior. She gives thanks for her part in God's great plan, but her song sounds more like the trumpet of a prophet than the simple celebration of a grateful parent-to-be, for she understands herself and the son she carries as central characters in God's liberating activity in the world.

God "has shown strength with his arm," she proclaims, and "he has scattered the proud in the thoughts of their hearts." God has "brought down the powerful from their thrones, and lifted up the lowly," thus setting on end human conventions of greatness and political power. God "has filled the hungry with good things, and sent the rich away empty," thus challenging our assumptions about economic measures of value. "He has helped his servant Israel," by bringing the people a Savior in their time of bondage. Mary's song moves beyond sentimentality to declare Jesus' coming as an advent of great political importance. By doing so, she identifies herself as a political actor and the opening voice in the resistance movement to establish the reign of God on earth. She too embodies the righteous commitment to mothering as an act of political resistance to unjust power.

I think a lot about political virtues these days, the traits of character in citizens and leaders that make for a healthy democratic society. In my writing and teaching, I tend to focus on civility, a set of virtues that allows us to navigate disagreement in a pluralistic society like ours with respect and grace.[1] But the calendar's invitation to think about Mother's Day has me thinking that mothering too represents a set of virtues that may be essential to a healthy society, making the role of mother important not just to our families but to society as a whole. Think of the virtues we associate with mothering at its best, in the ideal: unconditional love; deep investment in the good of other human beings; an impulse to provide for others, to protect others; reliability; strength; nurturing; self-sacrifice; and drawing happiness from others' happiness. Are these not an apt description of what it means to be human at our best? Are these not the virtues that we Christians most associate with Jesus Christ, our quintessential model for living a life for God and others? Do these not strike us as character traits that, if nurtured in citizens and leaders more deliberately, would make us a healthier society? Like civility, perhaps mothering symbolizes a set of virtues we would do well to encourage as the bedrock of a better-functioning society.

To be sure, we could expand our focus on mothers to parents and guardians more generally, to argue that these same virtues are ideally displayed by, say, fathers to their children. But in this particular time we are living in, when habits of grotesque hyper-masculinity are exposed from the shadows, when some powerful men are finally being made to account for their abuse of women while others evade justice, associating these virtues specifically with women who inhabit the role of mother stands as a particularly potent contrast to politics and power as usual in this country.[2] The virtues of mothering stand in judgment of destructive behavior we have ignored in the past or are normalizing in our present. The practice of

---

1. Davis, *In Defense of Civility*.

2. I have in mind here the sordid tales of famous and powerful men behaving badly in the worlds of entertainment, politics, and finance—men like Bill Cosby, Harvey Weinstein, Jeffrey Epstein, and of course, President Donald J. Trump.

mothering stands as an act of resistance to a culture of disrespect, dehu-manization, and violence. The virtues of mothering remind us what it means ideally to be human: to be invested in others, to help and nurture one another, to assume the best of one another, to give, to share, to help, and to encourage. Actual mothers—and fathers and grandparents and guard-ians—raise us to do and care about these things. They cultivate in us and pass on to us healthy moral and social traditions. They make us capable of being good in our relationships and responsible in our citizenship. They raise us to be good human beings.

If mothering—and by extension, parenting—is such a good, not just for domestic family life but for the life of the nation and the world, then we should celebrate it, not just as a private choice for individual fulfillment but as a contribution to the common good. And if parenting is so valuable to the common good, we should not only celebrate it but also support it. That means investing in stronger economic safety nets for women and children, because we recognize investment in family security contributes to national and global security. It means we get with the program and standardize paid parental leave, so women in particular do not need to choose between car-ing for their new children and keeping their jobs. It means flexibility in the workplace, childcare at the office, adoption benefits, and taking advantage of technology to creatively challenge assumptions about when and from where we must work. It means vigorously protecting every woman's right and prerogative to determine when she is ready to assume this socially vital role of parent. It means an end to the choices we demand (sometimes ex-plicitly, often implicitly) from women between professional progression and having a family.

For mothering—parenting—is not just a domestic experience but an act of citizenship and a contribution to the common good. And the virtues that mothers ideally reflect are an increasingly rare glimpse into an alterna-tive to the destructive political culture that currently surrounds us. So like Moses' cunning mother and Jesus' prophetic one, let us commit to raising our children as an act of resistance. Let those of us who are mothers and fathers, grandparents, guardians—indeed the church as a surrogate family of faith—double down on responsibility to our children, through which we teach a better way and hope and labor for a better future. Good parenting subverts the inhumanities of the present by investing in our children, for in their futures we hope for brighter glimpses of the kingdom of God.

8

The End of War

(Memorial Day)

"The war to end war," or "the war to end all wars" (as we commonly remember the phrase), was how Woodrow Wilson ambitiously and optimistically justified World War I. He hoped war would establish global peace (and US dominance) and abolish the need for war in the future. His hope was met with considerable cynicism at the time, and ever since it has been invoked as a sardonic lament. Memorial Day after Memorial Day, now a century after the conclusion of World War I, we are reminded by our commemorations that it ended nothing. The culmination of that conflict directly contributed to the rise of the Second World War, the end of which fed the conflicts in Korea and Southeast Asia, which spurred superpower interventions in the Middle East, and on and on and on. World War I ended nothing; instead it contributed to the bloodiest century in human history.

The persistence of war in our world prompts a perennial question for Christians: Should people of faith hope for an end to war in human history? Is that even possible? Is war a scourge to eliminate or a necessary evil that we endure or sometimes even utilize for good causes? Should we Christians be categorically opposed to the use of violence and war in the name of justice and peace, or should we resign ourselves to its necessity?

Many Christians today believe pacifism is the heart of the gospel. They take their cue from the Prince of Peace who rode into Jerusalem on a humble donkey, preaching love for enemies and turning the other cheek to the point of surrendering to the cross. They hear the apostle Paul advise Romans Christians long ago to bless persecutors and refuse to repay evil with evil (Rom 12:14–21), and they take those words as a gospel ethic. From its very beginning, Christian community has included people of faith who reject violence as antithetical to the gospel.

Pacifists like Martin Luther King Jr. embraced Christ's teaching that we should love our enemies. Whether he was talking about domestic conflict or international affairs, King rejected the use of violence in the struggle for justice. He argued Christians should labor with a different spirit for what is right and good, a radical love defined this way:

> Agape [is] understanding and creative, redemptive goodwill for all men. An overflowing love which seeks nothing in return, agape is the love of God operating in the human heart. At this level, we love men not because we like them, nor because their ways appeal to us, nor even because they possess some type of divine spark; we love every man because God loves him. At this level, we love the person who does an evil deed, although we hate the deed that he does.[1]

Hate "scars the soul and distorts" us, King claimed. Hate fails to reconcile us with our enemy, but it also changes us destructively. By contrast, "love is the only force capable of transforming an enemy into a friend," King insisted.[2] Hate tears down relationships, but love transforms them and redeems them.

In the spirit of this ethic of love, King advocated for nonviolent solutions to human conflict. He recognized his commitment to nonviolence was countercultural. The dominant moral ethos says you fight force with force. Someone hits you, and you hit back. But King insisted Christians are called to do something different:

> My friends, we have followed the so-called practical way for too long a time now, and it has led inexorably to deeper confusion and chaos. Time is cluttered with the wreckage of communities which surrendered to hatred and violence. For the salvation of our nation and the salvation of mankind, we must find another way . . . To our bitter opponents we say: "We shall match your capacity to inflict suffering by our capacity to endure suffering.

1. King, *Strength to Love*, 52.
2. King, *Strength to Love*, 53.

> We shall meet your physical force with soul force. Do to us what
> you will, and we shall continue to love you . . . One day we shall
> win freedom, but not only for ourselves. We shall so appeal to
> your heart and conscience that we shall win you in the process,
> and our victory will be a double victory."[3]

King embraced the countercultural nature of his ethic of loving non-violence, for to his mind it was the faithful Christian way.

The commitment to loving the enemy underwrote King's insistence on nonviolent civil disobedience in the struggle against segregation in the US, but it also informed his approach to international affairs. "No individual can live alone," he preached one Christmas morning. "No nation can live alone, and as long as we try, the more we are going to have war in this world. Now the judgment of God is upon us, and we must either learn to live together as brothers or we are all going to perish together as fools."[4] King endorsed redemptive goodwill for all people, even our enemies, because Jesus commanded it, but also because to King's mind it was the only tactic that ultimately would work to create a global society of justice and reconciliation. He rejected the charge that his emphasis on love made his social program utopian or idealistic. He thought loving the enemy was a profoundly realistic and pragmatic approach to social and global conflict, and the only option we have left, for history already has demonstrated the futility of violence. King's Christian faith permitted him to imagine a better future for the world: "With this faith we will be able to speed up the day when there will be peace on earth and good will toward men. It will be a glorious day, the morning stars will sing together, and the sons of God will shout for joy."[5]

Not all Christians share King's pacifism, however. Some Christians believe war is sometimes necessary to pursue justice or care for the vulnerable. They support use of the military when it is justified, and in fact many Christians serve in the armed forces without an ounce of moral contradiction.[6] They understand Jesus' apparently violent reaction to corruption in the temple (John 2:13–16) as divine indication that sometimes anger and violence serve a righteous cause. They hear in Paul's reminder to be subject

3. King, *Strength to Love,* 56.

4. King, "Christmas Sermon on Peace," 253.

5. King, "Christmas Sermon on Peace," 258.

6. Contrary to the common way Christian history is told, the early church was not unambiguously pacifist. Evidence suggests Christians served in the Roman army from the earliest days of the church, and that Christian leaders were of mixed mind on the compatibility between Christian faith and violent state action. For an especially accessible introduction to the history of pacifism and just war thinking in Christian thought, see Cahill, *Love Your Enemies.*

to authority (Rom 13) an assurance that government and its military can be the means by which God's justice is meted out.

Reinhold Niebuhr was an important Christian thinker and public intellectual of the twentieth century. Writing in the period between the two world wars, Niebuhr observed liberal church leaders actively and ambitiously calling for an end to all war. They bought into Wilson's promise that World War I would be that end of all war. They hoped in the promise of the League of Nations to create alternative mechanisms for nations to adjudicate their differences, so they would not have to resort to war. They invested heavily in nonviolent visions of a world order. Niebuhr was surrounded by good Christians advocating for the end of war, and he dismissed virtually all of them.

In an influential essay entitled "Why the Christian Church Is Not Pacifist," Niebuhr claimed most forms of Christian pacifism are, in fact, heresy. Niebuhr was not using the term *heresy* as it was invoked in medieval times, suggesting that Christian pacifists should be thrown out of the church or burned at the stake. He was using the term evocatively to make his point that pacifism is not an accurate reflection of the Christian gospel. Niebuhr thought pacifism is heresy because in truth it is based on an unjustified optimism in humanity's moral potential for goodness. Christian calls to end war imply human beings are virtuous enough to pull it off, but Niebuhr asserted that Christianity presumes no such thing. In fact, Christianity assumes human beings always possess a penchant for pursuing their own self-interests at the expense of others, especially when they act in numbers (that is, as societies). As a result of this tendency to egoism, we always will fail to live up to God's ideals and expectations for us. According to Niebuhr, Christian liberals of his day had forgotten one important conviction of Christian theology, a little idea called sin.

Niebuhr thought all those Christians who called for a world devoid of war and thought it was a realistic possibility during the so-called "Christian Century" were spouting not good Christian doctrine but heretical Renaissance humanism, or an Enlightenment-based optimism in the moral progress of humanity. If we just spread the Christian religion more broadly, they told us, if we just educate people more successfully, we will evolve out of our need for violence. Niebuhr thought such an optimism was undercut by historical experience and the testament of Christian faith, which reminds us we are good creatures but also tragically self-defeating, and thus we will never live up to the ideals we or God have cast for ourselves. No society can be constructed on a pure ethic of love—not even close. "The good news of the gospel," Niebuhr wrote, "is not the law that we ought to love one another," which Niebuhr believed was an ideal that the doctrine of sin teaches us is unattainable for human societies. "The good news of the gospel is that there is a resource of divine mercy which is able to overcome a contradiction within our own souls, which we cannot overcome ourselves."[7] A perfect human society of peace and justice is an impossibility, so we Christians should stop expecting one. Instead, we rely on the mercies of God when we inevitably fail to live up to God's desires of peace and justice. Grace, not moral perfection, is the Christian gospel.

Does this mean the Christian message of love is irrelevant to world affairs? Niebuhr believed the Christian gospel of love is essential to world affairs, but not as a governing principle to implement. We cannot create a society that exhibits perfect goodwill, but we can work for something closer to the ideal than our current political and economic systems exhibit. Thus, the gospel of love serves as a plumb line by which we measure and improve our efforts at a just society. The Christian message of love reminds us of the impossible possibility toward which we labor. The Christian gospel of love serves as a measure of our efforts to strive for more peace and justice than we currently enjoy. It helps us evaluate better and worse social systems and structures, even while reminding us that none of our efforts will perfectly live up to its measurement. Love gives us a goal toward which to labor, even while reminding us of a perfection of virtue that will forever elude us.

War as a reflection of our collective moral failings will always be with us, reminded Niebuhr. In fact, sometimes we will need to employ violence and war for the work of justice and peace. Sometimes war has a regrettable but necessary purpose, to act on behalf of those who languish under the oppression of others. Sometimes not intervening in Nazi or Rwandan genocide or Syrian domestic terrorism, for instance, will turn out to be a greater evil than committing acts of violence to keep innocents from harm's way.[8] For Niebuhr, King's call for a "beloved community" of peace and redemptive goodwill was unjustifiably optimistic. Christians who take seriously the law of love and the need for grace expect something different: a world

---

7. Niebuhr, "Why the Christian Church Is Not Pacifist," 302.

8. The "just war tradition" is a legacy of moral reflection on the circumstances under which war may be a regrettable but ethical response to aggression or oppression. It is deeply rooted in Christian tradition, in the writings of Augustine, Thomas Aquinas, and others. The idea of morally justified war has plenty of critics. Some argue that just war thinking does not offer the coherent ethical analysis it claims, but rather provides a convenient vocabulary for the political justification of imperial aggression (often after the fact) against less-powerful nations and communities. I do not deny that just war thinking often is used this way, especially in popular political rhetoric, but I still believe that the historical tradition of principled reflection on war is subtle and sophisticated enough to help us in contemporary consideration of global conflict.

in which we struggle for better approximations of the beloved community, while confessing our inevitable failures to achieve it.

Both King and Niebuhr claimed to be giving voice to the gospel's relevance to political and international affairs. Both King and Niebuhr claimed their expectations for human society were realistic and faithful. So which one was right? Personally, I find myself caught between the two, convinced that each of them possessed a kernel of truth. The success of the civil rights movement seems to vindicate King's call to nonviolence, but the persistence of human rights atrocities in our time suggests Niebuhr's lower regard for the human condition was more accurate. King undeniably channeled the teachings of Jesus in his call to love our enemies and meet brute force with soul force. Niebuhr, though, also appealed to deeply rooted Christian themes in his emphasis on the reality of sin, the need for grace, and the wisdom in tempering our expectations of justice from any human society.

Which one was right? Should Christians hope for the end of war? Is that hope realistic? Is it faithful? At the end of the day, I tend to subscribe to Niebuhr's realism. Memorial Day annually chastens any excessive optimism I harbor, for the injustice and oppression against which our soldiers fought seems too persistent to expect a global reign of peace and love any time soon. In the spirit of both Niebuhr and King, however, perhaps we might also say this: in the face of persistent human destructiveness, we followers of the Way of Jesus are called to strive purposefully toward *more* peace in the world. Perhaps at the very least Niebuhr and King would agree Christians should witness to a radical, countercultural peace that judges, challenges, and reshapes human efforts at creating a just society, here in our nation and in the world. They may disagree about how close we can get to the ideal, but I think they would both agree we ought to labor toward it. In a global climate in which division, hatred, violence, and demonization are stoked to entrenched habit, the gospel can help prevent the world from getting numb to it all. Allegiance to the Way of Jesus gives us strength to love, even if imperfectly. That imperfect witness to love is sorely needed as long as the end of war remains stubbornly elusive.

9

The Importance of Being Father

(Father's Day)

Truth be told, after fifteen years of fatherhood, I still do not know how to think about myself in the context of this day. Father's Day does not feel like it is about me, at least not intuitively. On Father's Day I reflect on my own father. I remember the very good times with my dad, moments that in some ways get more poignant as he and I get older and the relationship roles reverse just a bit. I reminisce about deer hunting and wood stacking and the hundreds of projects I "helped" him to complete—little more than a chattering go-fer as a boy, but absorbing practical knowledge I would not fully appreciate until I was an adult and father myself. I think about the ways I am shaped by being the son of an Appalachian coal miner, influences that go down to my core, accidental on his part, but molding who I am as a person and as a professional. These days I spend a little of Father's Day telling myself I will be more faithful this year in calling home and visiting. On Father's Day, I think like a son. It continues to catch me a bit by surprise that this day could also be about me.

And yet, being a father is who I am, and with every passing year it becomes as formative to my character as being a son. My sense of self and my responsibilities in this life are defined in large part from the duties of parenthood; my calendar certainly reflects that I have two jobs now. I think as a father now, too. In the classroom, I approach many of the ethical issues I teach with different eyes. In the airport, my heart beats faster when I hear a small voice crying, even though neither of my children is that small and vulnerable anymore. I know more about issues we broadly refer to as "special needs" than I ever did before. I am more invested and interested in a place and culture on the other side of the world (where my sons were born) than before two boys named Jae and Kisung became my joy and responsibility. I watch basketball and NASCAR races and I know a little about the martial arts; as it turns out, there are sports other than football played in this country. I am father now.

Still, this day surprises me, revealing that on a day that celebrates fathers, I do not think of myself deliberately as its subject, even though that role has fundamentally reshaped who I have become in the last fifteen years. I wonder if I have not successfully internalized my identity as parent because I do not think I am nearly as good in that role as I am in the others I occupy. The response to my books by editors and readers seems to suggest I am a pretty good writer. Positive course evaluations reassure me I am a good teacher. Unless my congregational friends are just being kind (a distinct possibility!), I have game as a preacher.

But parenthood? I am far from the head of the class on that front. I work too much. I hear stories of parents who "never miss one of the kids' games," and I know immediately that I fall short. I am not where I should be when I should be. I am impatient and can be emotionally distant. I am naturally wired to spend more time alone than with other people. I am still working on molding my strong personality and genetic deficiencies to the requirements of parenthood, to meet my kids where they are, where they need me to be, to be the reliable support each of them needs in climbing the hills that stand before them.

The idea of fatherhood—of parenthood—is problematic for many of us. For some, like me, it evokes our own shortcomings. For others, it triggers reminders of parents who have failed us, sometimes in traumatically injurious ways. And while parental failures are possible from mothers, too—as anyone who has read or seen *Mommie Dearest* knows—the history of fatherhood is even spottier. It comes with the legacy of patriarchy, domination, absence, misogyny, and abuse. For many, the concept of fatherhood is morally ambivalent at best.

That is part of the reason why more and more Christians have such a hard time using the language of "father" to refer to God. Reference to God as Father is embedded in that classical Christian formulation of God as Trinity, and these days both the parental language for God and the Three-in-One conceptual gymnastics are contested ideas, even among Christians.

But the idea of Trinity and its gendered language for the first Person has deep roots in our theological tradition, so they are not easily jettisoned. As Matthew tells it, the Great Commission of Jesus' disciples after his death was to go and recruit followers, not just to the cult of Jesus of Nazareth, but to a life lived in allegiance to the Father, Son, and Holy Spirit. Picking a fight with Father God or the Trinity can feel like the foundations of faith are crumbling beneath us.

We are well served to remember Christians invoked the Father, Son, and Holy Spirit long before they were quite sure how the three related to one another. In this seemingly contradictory invocation, they struggled to maintain the Jewish monotheistic confession of one God and yet insist that Jesus was a manifestation of God, and that the enduring presence of the Spirit was also a manifestation of God. Christian thinkers spent an awful lot of time in the church's early period trying to make sense of how both of these ideas could be true: God is one and God is three. In fact, the church has never stopped trying to make sense of it, though in the fourth and fifth centuries certain formulations began to get official traction—formulations millions of Christians recite each Sunday in the Nicene Creed or Apostles' Creed.

Even in those creeds, Christians were not entirely sure what they were saying, and while this traditional Trinity language has come to dominate Christian worship in the Western world, many Christians find it problematic. Some reject it because they find the Nicene concepts unhelpful in our time and place. But many more reject it because of the first part: Father. To refer to God as Father, as the church has for centuries, invests our understanding of God with the very real baggage that comes with bad fatherhood. To talk of God as Father tempts us to think of God as an old white man who sits in brutal authority over the world. As feminist thinker Mary Daly argued, we need to move "beyond God the Father" because that language encourages us to see God as a stereotypical man, acting principally through the options of violence, vengeance, and punishment.[1] God as a kind of misogynistic and oppressive father endorses patriarchy and underwrites men's domination of human society. For many people, talking of God as Father is not only less useful, it is downright harmful.

Those who reject Father-God talk sometimes suggest we substitute "Mother" in referring to that aspect of the Holy Trinity. I actually like that quite a bit; it is biblical imagery as well, and it maintains the relational intention of Trinity language while infusing it with a significant social and

---

1. Daly, *Beyond God the Father*.

theological corrective.[2] But even to talk of Mother-Child-Spirit instead of Father-Son-Spirit does not get you away from the negative connotations that parental language can have—authoritarianism, abuse, neglect. Because humans are imperfect, *any* parental language can encourage negative associations with God, leading some Christians to prefer alternative wording altogether, like Creator-Redeemer-Sustainer.[3]

But on this Father's Day, I wonder if the only way to respond to the liabilities in Trinity-talk is to move beyond the Father, as Daly suggests. Is the only healthy response to its shortcomings to dispense altogether with the traditional metaphor? For many of us, parental metaphors carry important *positive* connotations, too. Dependable care, unconditional love, wisdom, patience, and trust are ideals we associate with good parenting that also might describe how we experience God in the world and in our lives. This may seem like a silly example, but one of my earliest childhood memories is of walking in the woods with my dad and his favorite beagle, Spotty. On that day, Spotty accidentally stuck her nose in a yellow jacket nest in the ground, and before we knew it those hornets were all over her, Dad, and me. I remember my dad bending down and picking that dog up with one arm and me with the other and running out of the woods, with strength, swiftness, and a disregard for his own well-being.[4] That reliable and sacrificial strength in the face of need works as a reassuring divine analogy for me.

My point is that there are virtues to parenthood that might make useful (if approximate) images for how we experience God in our lives. If that is true, then talking of God as Father and Mother perhaps is not all bad. But it is also true that our actual experiences of parenthood—being parents or having them—often fall short of those ideals. Perhaps even here, though,

---

2. See Isaiah 42:14, 49:15, and 66:13 for examples of maternal metaphors for God. In addition, Hosea 13:8 describes God as a mother bear who viciously reacts against a threat to her cubs. In the New Testament, Jesus compares God's yearning for a wayward Jerusalem to a hen calling for her chicks (Matt 23:37).

3. Count me among those who are dissatisfied with the substitution of Creator-Redeemer-Sustainer for the traditional Father-Son-Holy Spirit, especially in worship. The two formulas simply do not describe the same thing. The former describes the *work* of God, or the ways in which God operates in the world. The latter is a description of how God *relates* to Godself, as well as an attempt to capture different ways in which God relates to us. Both formulas capture something important to a Christian conception of God, but they are not interchangeable, despite what is implied by the substitution, especially common in liberal-leaning churches concerned about the patriarchal language in the classical Trinity formulation.

4. Interestingly, I had opportunity to relive this paternal feat when my son Jae was about the same age and accidently aggravated a hornet's nest in a friend's yard. Unlike my father, however, I tripped and fell while whisking my son away from danger, a symbol of my lifelong struggle to live into the standards of fatherhood.

the use of parental language for God can be helpful. Sallie McFague reminds us that theology employs metaphors as approximate comparisons between the divine and the human—not an equation but an approximation, where something significant is said both by the similarities between the image and its object *and* by the disconnect between image and object.[5] Father-God talk and Mother-God talk give us imagistic language through which to emphasize certain qualities to the experience of God's presence in our lives. At the same time, there are ways that parenthood—in the imperfect way we experience and practice it—fails to capture who we profess God to be. But in those moments when we are reminded of the challenges and disappointments in human parenthood, the metaphor still teaches us something about God and parenting. The disconnect we experience between God the Father and our experiences of human fathers simply reinforces for us the greatness of God while also suggesting a helpful measure for our all-too-human attempts at parenting. God as loving Father serves as the ideal to which all of us imperfect fathers, mothers, grandparents, and guardians strive.

Indeed, it is possible that using parenthood as a metaphor for God can help redeem the concept of parenthood itself, by shining a more gracious light on it. Referring to the God of Jesus as Parent provides a plumb line for what it means for us to be parents. Giving parenthood theological symbolic significance elevates the language above the imperfections we experience and inspires us to think more highly of the calling to be mother or father, parent, grandparent, or guardian. Striving to be parents under the watch of the one we call Parent also reassures us with the expectation of grace to forgive ourselves when we fall short. Confessing God as Parent reminds us to receive forgiveness and unconditional love as well as to give it, to be relieved of the burden to be perfect, and to embrace the virtue in the striving. Confessing God as Parent reminds us that parenthood, like the Christian life, is always a work in progress to be embraced with prayerful enthusiasm, not with dread and fear of failure.

In these ways, talking of God as Father or Mother gives parenthood holy significance. It encourages us to see it as religious vocation, as a calling that some of us undertake with joy and nervousness. In my case, being father is every bit as important to the person I have been called to be as the vocations of teacher, preacher, and writer, even if—or perhaps especially because—I am more naturally gifted for those other roles than I am for being Dad. I have had to work hard at being the dad I am called to be, and I need grace in the many instances when I fail to live up to my calling. The process of try/fail/try again simply makes being father an appropriate part

---

5. McFague, *Models of God*, x–xi.

of the imperfect Christian striving to which God has invited me. Reliance on God the Father reminds me of the good I aspire to in this role, while it also assures me I am loved and forgiven when I miss the mark.

With my two children more than halfway to adulthood, it is probably past time for me to get comfortable with the fact that Father's Day is about me too. It is a day of affirmation and encouragement for all of us who embrace the holy calling to raise children and help them become good people who love themselves and others as God loves us. That holy duty is hard, and none of us discharges it perfectly. That certainly describes me, but as I strive to live into this awesome responsibility, I am sure I am a better dad for the template my father—and my Father—set for me.

10

Rest and Recreation

(First Day of Summer)

If the TV commercials that inevitably run from May through September are any indication, summertime is the season for sandy beaches and citrus-laced beer, naps in hammocks that swing gently in artificially green yards, and off-roading treks in a brand-new SUV. Summer is the season of leisure, popular culture tells us, and even if our vacations struggle to live up to the aspirations in those ads (in part because most of us cannot afford to regularly purchase all of the beer or vehicles they try to sell us), many folks look forward to the long and warm days of summer to get away from the stress or doldrums of work. One reason summer is such an anticipated respite from work, though, is because many of us struggle to get away from our labors for most of the rest of the year. I am a teacher, and for those of us who work in education the academic year can be relentless and oppressive; it offers few opportunities to take even a "mental health day," let alone escape for a week to the Bahamas. But at least I get the summer, when the pace slows considerably at my school and there is time for family, play, and rest.

Truth be told, though, I struggle with even the downtime of summer. I am not very good at relaxing, and in that way I am an apt reflection of the culture that produced me. Despite the impression the summer commercials leave, Americans do not value rest as much as they do work. Work is our

74

currency of value, the byproduct of capitalism's domination of our cultural ethos. The sociologist Max Weber famously argued that Calvinism may be responsible for the success of capitalism and its insatiable work ethic in the West.[1] According to Weber, capitalism flourished in Europe and America where Calvinism's celebration of unrequited productivity underwrote the cycles of production and investment necessary for capitalism. Calvinists like our American Puritan forefathers taught that work is an important good, a virtue and vocation and opportunity for God's blessing. Industry could serve as God's delight with us as well as an expression of our gratitude for divine favor, so those early Calvinists encouraged the pious to work as hard as possible. But those same Calvinists also vehemently resisted lavish living, which presented a moral dilemma when good Christians were diligent and responsible to their work and began to see yield from their industriousness. Work as hard as you can, said the Calvinists, but do not spend all that money on yourself. What is a budding industrialist to do, though, if he follows the Calvinist work ethic to great success but then must minimize the luxury made possible by the riches of all that productivity? If you cannot spend it, you reinvest it, and from this Calvinist cocktail of industry and thrift is capitalism born.

Although generally I think the Puritans get a bad rap in our cultural memory, it may be true that our American obsession with work is a legitimate Puritan hangover. Most of us are familiar with the culture of busyness that imbues American society. Many people are busy working jobs that ask us to do more than reasonable work hours permit. We busily raise our kids, all the while accidentally (or sometimes intentionally) modeling this ethic of busyness for their emulation, as evidenced by our children's common overcommitment to curricular and extracurricular activities. Busyness defines how we relate to one another, for it now serves as the standard greeting between friends; we routinely respond to another's benign "How are you?" with a litany of all the responsibilities weighing on us. Busyness even redefines how we think about recreation, pushing us to play as hard as we work, to the point that weekend schedules furiously resemble the exhausting work week from which they are supposed to be a respite. Busyness has become our American measure of human value, of ourselves and of others.

Our worship of work shapes our understanding of social issues, none more than the economic inequality we now take for granted in this country. There is a long history in the United States of assuming the poor are poor because they do not work as hard as we do. Our Puritan forefathers talked about the "idle poor," distinguishing people who are accidentally poor from

---

1. See Weber, *Protestant Ethic and the Spirit of Capitalism.*

those whose poverty stems from their lack of discipline or drive. These days we still derogatively refer to "welfare moms" to capture a similar category of people whose poverty results from their own character flaws, and unlike the older term, this contemporary phrase includes sexist and racist undertones. Insinuations that the poor are poor because they do not work hard enough conveniently distract us from the systemic causes of inequality that create the circumstances that give rise to poverty. The judgmentalism that drips from simplistic depictions of welfare recipients ignores the reality that the wage rate of most Americans has stagnated or declined over the last fifty years, while a very small percentage of people have become exponentially wealthier. Poverty is not simply a reflection of bad character on the part of the poor; systemic injustice, excessive governmental deregulation, poor health care, the demise of union representation, and good old-fashioned bad luck also contribute to poverty. The American Dream still spins a fictional narrative, however, that if you simply work hard you can make something of yourself in this country. Our idolatry of work is baked into the DNA of the United States, shaping our understanding of who we are as a nation.

The celebration of busyness and productivity has become part of the American moral worldview, and because of this cultural worship of busyness, we often find it difficult to take time off, for doing so feels countercultural, irresponsible, and honestly kind of lame. I certainly see myself in this little bit of cultural seduction. Perhaps because I have bought into the American mythos too naively, or perhaps because I spend too much time reading Puritans, I find it very difficult to be idle. I have lost the ability to relax. My spouse Elizabeth says I border on the pathological with the way I stress about not using every minute of the day efficiently. Some of my pathology is rooted in my job, especially in the years I invested in various kinds of college administration, when there simply was not enough time to do all that was demanded of my colleagues and me. But my inability to relax goes back further, to undergraduate and graduate school days spent desperately beating back the feelings of intellectual inferiority and cultural displacement that come with being a first-generation college student. As an Appalachian hillbilly in the elite culture of higher education, I have spent much of my professional life fighting imposter syndrome, trying to prove my worth by outworking the people around me. That unhealthy work ethic regularly bleeds into my off time too; I have anxiety attacks when I feel like I am sitting around for any length of time, and before I know it I am turning fun home projects into time trials that need to be checked off a to-do list as soon as possible. Perhaps Elizabeth is right; I am pathological. That must be why she let me get a motorcycle.

But this kind of allergy to rest, even when it does not rise to my extreme, is not healthy. Study after study tells us rest makes us physically and psychologically healthier. More sleep gives us more energy and lowers our chance of heart disease, stroke, and mental health problems. More rest makes us more productive, so even from the perspective of our American celebration of productivity, we ought to value rest as something that makes us better workers, creators, and producers. Beyond making us better economic actors, though, rest also makes us better people, by giving us more time with each other to bond as neighbors and communities. For makers and consumers and plain ol' human beings, rest has real practical benefit.

Rest and recreation also are religious goods and sacred gifts. The Ten Commandments sometimes get a bad rap among liberal Christians like myself, because they seem to dissolve the religious life into oppressive legalism, but I think the accusation sells the commandments short. What these commandments were meant to do was help define the community of ancient Israel, and they continue to function that way for us, if we let them. What does it mean to be a community of people faithful to God and to each other? The Ten Commandments offer parameters and expectations for a moral society, which may be one reason that versions of the Ten Commandments show up in religious traditions besides Judaism and Christianity. They are a bare-bones list of the things that make for a good community.

In the Hebrew Bible, the Ten Commandments actually appear in two places, in the book of Exodus and the book of Deuteronomy. Interestingly, in the midst of laws outlawing self-serving idolatry, murder, and theft appears the positive commendation of collective rest. "You shall observe the Sabbath, and make it holy" (Deut 5:12, my translation). If the commandments provide the basic contours of a good society, then the Bible indicates that opportunity for periodic rest is a fundamental ingredient for that good society. Rest, as ritualized in the idea of a Sabbath, is an essential human good and a sign of faithfulness. The requirement of a Sabbath implies that failure to rest is not just missed opportunity or unhealthy, but a moral and religious dereliction, an unwillingness to live the life God invites us to live. And a society that does not provide for the freedom to rest for all dehumanizes its citizens. In a culture that constantly equates goodness with productivity, the Sabbath imperative is a profoundly countercultural claim on us.

As is usually the case with biblical imperatives, the richness of this theological nugget on Sabbath is not in the straightforward requirement but its justification. Why is Sabbath important? Why is rest so highly valued that it is included in the top ten list of ways godly people ought to behave? Again, there are actually two versions of the Ten Commandments in the Bible, and while the commandments themselves are fairly consistent, their accompanying explanations are sometimes different, and we learn something from the variations between the Exodus and Deuteronomy versions. In Exodus, the writer insists that the people keep the Sabbath because God did:

> Remember the sabbath day, and keep it holy. Six days you shall labor and do all your work. But the seventh day is a sabbath to the LORD your God; you shall not do any work—you, your son or your daughter, your male or female slave, your livestock, or the alien resident in your towns. For in six days the LORD made heaven and earth, the sea, and all that is in them, but rested the seventh day; therefore the LORD blessed the sabbath day and consecrated it. (Exod 20:8–11)

By linking Sabbath with God's mythic acts in creation, we are reminded of the importance of the literal meaning of "re-creation." The ode to creation in the book of Genesis includes a stanza on God's seventh day, after "God saw everything that he had made, and indeed, it was very good," when "God finished the work that he had done" and "rested on the seventh day" from God's creative flurry (Gen 1:31—2:3). Did God literally rest on a seventh day? Like the majority of Jews and Christians, I do not read this story in Genesis as literal play-by-play on how God created the universe. I am not even sure I philosophically buy the idea that God *needs* to rest. But the creation song in Genesis seems to be saying that after all of the creative work, God took some time to enjoy what God had done. God celebrated the goodness God had made by resting, bathing in the beauty and order that just emanated from God's loving intent. In keeping Sabbath, then, we commemorate that divine creativity and its celebration, and in the process live into our calling to be *imago Dei*, creatures who reflect the likeness and habits of their God. Sabbath becomes holy time to mimic the divine as we were meant to do, including the divine penchant to take respite in something that brings us joy. In this way, the divine endorsement of Sabbath is a way of saying we are built for rest, for we were designed to be children of God.

The approach that Deuteronomy takes to the Sabbath is different, but no less revealing. In Deuteronomy, the text depicts God commanding the Sabbath as a perpetual reminder of God's liberation of the Hebrew people from Egypt:

> Observe the sabbath day and keep it holy, as the LORD your God commanded you. Six days you shall labor and do all your work. But the seventh day is a sabbath to the LORD your God; you shall not do any work—you, or your son or your daughter, or your male or female slave, or your ox or your donkey, or any of your livestock, or the resident alien in your towns, so that your

male and female slave may rest as well as you. Remember that
you were a slave in the land of Egypt, and the LORD your God
brought you out from there with a mighty hand and an out-
stretched arm; therefore the LORD your God commanded you
to keep the sabbath day. (Deut 5:12–15)

In this version, the emphasis is on Sabbath as a moral commitment
rooted in a declaration of trust in God. God has taken care of God's people
before, so God will take care of us tomorrow, even if we take time off from
our labors. The commandment reminds us the world does not spin on the
axis of our own exertion, a message that puts into helpful context the absur-
dity of our current insatiable drive to be productive. Perhaps more importantly, Deuteronomy demands we see Sabbath not just as personal behavior
but also as a commitment to social justice. Concern for others is part of
the Sabbath command, including those who labor on our behalf. Again, if
the Ten Commandments represent a kind of skeletal structure for a good
society, then Deuteronomy suggests an essential part of that good society is
concern for the basic human need for and right to rest, as a reflection of the
liberating grace God extends to us. With respect to God's history of liberation, Deuteronomy's version of the commandments suggests a good society
should strive for a program of rest that is inclusive and liberating.

This interpretation of Sabbath as social justice is also important in our
time and place, for the truth is that Americans' failure to rest is not entirely
a result of individual acquiescence to the idolatry of work. It is equally true
that many in our society do not rest because they cannot afford to take time
off. Inequality and the threat of poverty deprive many people of the good of
rest. Many Americans work more than one job just to approach the federal
poverty line. Many people are working long days and weekends because the
sensible gains of labor unions in the middle part of the last century (fighting
for the minimum wage and the forty-hour work week, for instance) have
eroded under the pressures and policies of a globalized economy. As we are
recommitting to Sabbath rest in our individual lives for our own personal,
professional, and psychological good, Deuteronomy reminds us that a moral society works to ensure this basic human good for all people. Keeping the
Sabbath holy requires more from Christians than a personal commitment
to take it easy on Sundays. It requires us to advocate for social policies that
ensure all citizens can afford to live decent lives without working nearly
every hour of the day.

Walter Brueggemann argues the Sabbath was a community-defining
act of resistance among the Hebrew people of biblical times, and that it
similarly stands as a subversive act of resistance in our time and place:

Such faithful practice of work stoppage is an act of resistance. It declares in bodily ways that we will not participate in the anxiety system that pervades our social environment. We will not be defined by busyness and by acquisitiveness and by pursuit of more, in either our economics or our personal relations or anywhere in our lives. Because our life does not consist in commodity.[2]

By resting deliberately, with intention, we confess we are worth more than the yield of our labors. We have value because we are children of the Sabbath-taking and Sabbath-commanding God.

There may be legitimate reasons why most of us do not observe a specific day as Sabbath quite the way that our ancients did, with the total avoidance of labor from sunup to sundown. But the holy recommendation of regular rest is one we do well to heed, and for many of us it is a righteous project for which summer is particularly well suited. Rest makes us healthier, wealthier, and wiser, to be sure. More importantly, though, rest gives us time and energy to connect with one another and with God. And in that way, to indulge in regular rest is to witness against a culture of busyness and to testify to what is truly important, including the beauty of leisure as an authentic expression of our humanity and as a reflection of the divine.

2. Brueggemann, *Sabbath as Resistance*, 31. Brueggemann's wonderful little book offers an examination of the Sabbath through a close reading of Old Testament texts, considering the significance it had for the Hebrew community while powerfully suggesting ways in which this Jewish and Christian practice serves as a countercultural witness in our time and place.

11

For God and Country

(Fourth of July)

Each Fourth of July, Christian Americans face a question as old as our nation: What is the relationship between our profession of allegiance to Christ and our pledge of allegiance to the United States of America? What exactly does it mean to live in the confluence of those identities? Around this holiday, many of our congregations will sing national hymns while sharing our sanctuaries with the American flag, and some of us will listen to sermons redounding on the manifold ways God has blessed the United States of America. All of the patriotic religious pageantry suggests being Christian is easily compatible with expressions of patriotism. But is it that simple? Do love of country and Christian faithfulness fit together like two sides of a coin, or is there a fundamental disconnect between piety and patriotism that many Christian Americans simply choose to ignore? Is it even possible to be a Christian American and maintain integrity in both identities?

It is a great American tradition to collapse the two modifiers into one. Generations of politicians and church leaders have insisted the United States was founded as a Christian nation, and that the Founders intended for their new nation to govern by biblical principles and protect the Christian church as its soul. Today large segments of the population believe the term "Christian America" is redundant, for to be an American is obviously to live in a nation destined to be a "city on a hill" to the world, to witness to God and serve the name of Jesus Christ.[1] However popular an assumption that is, though, it is a gross oversimplification of American history. To talk of "Christian America" ignores the fact that our Founders were a complicated group of people, religiously speaking. They included traditional Christians but also philosophically minded people like Thomas Jefferson and James Madison, who were deeply suspicious of organized religion. The Founders included men motivated by religious vision but also leaders committed to the pursuit of life, liberty, and the pursuit of happiness for secular reasons. In the eyes of some Founders, what made America great was its faithfulness to Christian ideals, but to many other important leaders of the period, what made America great was its tolerance of religious difference and its commitment to the separation of faith and politics. Our founding was a cooperative effort of people of much faith, people of different faith, and people of very little faith in God.[2] Relatively few of them resembled the modern-day evangelicals who wistfully hearken back to the US's mythical Christian roots.

To collapse Christian identity and American citizenship is to tell bad history, but this erroneous account of America's founding is quite popular, and at times it has done enormous damage to our national conscience, for subscribing to this equation of Christian identity and American identity has implicated the United States in injustices against peoples who did not fit into that Christian narrative. The idea of a Christian nation helped to justify the annihilation of Native Americans in the early chapters of our national history, by depicting the original Americans as pagans incapable of trustworthy moral performance or civic loyalty. With a decidedly Protestant spin, the collapse of "Christian" into "American" also fed anti-Catholic sentiment through much of our history, as Catholics were not considered true or respectable Christians in the eyes of the Protestant majority. The religious tinge to our understanding of patriotism underwrote colonial expansion in the nineteenth and twentieth centuries, as well as the paternalism and

1. The description of the United States as a "city on a hill," serving as a beacon of freedom and democracy, was popularized by Ronald Reagan in the 1980s. The phrase originates, however, with Puritan John Winthrop, who invoked Jesus' Sermon on the Mount (Matt 5:14) to underscore the duty he believed the Massachusetts Bay Colony had to model a society based on Christian charity. As he made clear in a sermon allegedly preached on board the ship that carried him and a significant group of immigrants to the Massachusetts shore, the duty to model charity meant exhibiting faithfulness to God and loving commitment to one another and the common good. Winthrop was convinced that the American experiment would bring honor or derision upon God, depending on the colonists' faithfulness to one another. See Winthrop, "Model of Christian Charity."

2. Davis, *In Defense of Civility*, 24–31.

hostility with which we treated the "others" whom we encountered in co-lonial conquest. Well into the twentieth century, collapse of Christian and American interests may have contributed to Americans' slow response to German atrocities against Jews under Hitler, and the dark side of baptizing national identity remains today in the deep suspicion of Muslims that many good Christian Americans harbor. If you think national loyalty requires subscription to the Christian religion, then you may be concerned with the growth of American Muslim communities and the elevation of Muslims to political office, perhaps more than you are disturbed by, say, the deleterious impact of a nominally Christian president whose daily behavior flies in the face of all of those good Christian values that are allegedly so essential to the well-being of our national life.

Equating Christian commitment and patriotism is bad history, and it also is bad theology, for collapsing the two risks transforming one's nation from a wonderful gift of grace into an idol. "Thou shalt have no other gods before me" (Exod 20:3 KJV), warns the commandment, but when we col-lapse Christian faith with patriotism, we lose the ability to recognize the difference between God and Caesar, when obligation to God and demands of country do not travel in the same direction. At best, this results in a loss of critical perspective; we no longer are in a position to evaluate our nation's conformity to God's intentions, and so we act as if national policy is some-how immune from the moral obligations of the sovereign God. At worst, we succumb to the temptation to interpret God's will as whatever serves the national interests of the United States, at which point our allegiance to nation defines, judges, and limits our obligations to God. Nation becomes our highest god, above the God of Abraham, Isaac, and Jacob, and the com-mitment to being "Christian" is subsumed by the commitment to being "American." Put bluntly, to collapse being Christian into being American, to equate God's intentions for the world with American foreign or domestic interests, is nothing short of heresy. It remains, however, the most popular form of heresy affirmed in the US today.

In response to this heresy, some Christian thinkers have gone the other direction, emphasizing the ways Christian identity might move us in different directions than our national obligations, provoking us to call into question our loyalties to the state. Drawing on a deep heritage of coun-tercultural Christianity, one that goes back to the persecuted martyrs of the early church and the Anabaptists of the Reformation, these thinkers remind Christian Americans they are heirs to the kingdom of God before they are citizens of the political realm. Religious identity is primary, so it should be the lens through which we view our political obligations. A number of years ago, two prominent Methodist theologians, Stanley

Hauerwas and William Willimon, wrote a popular book called *Resident Aliens*, in which they cautioned against the heretical collapse of Christian and American values.[3] Inspired by 1 Peter's call for Christians to live in the land as "aliens and exiles," they called American Christians to consider themselves a holy and separate people and to commit to countercultural lives governed by faith principles. They urged Christians to be deeply suspicious of America's commitment to capitalism and to live in defiance of American foreign policy built on the fiction of morally justified violence. For Hauerwas and Willimon, to be a true Christian required Americans to live in but not belong to the culture of America, and to witness to the alternative politics of being church.

As helpful as this prophetic correction might be, however, a strident opposition between our Christian and American identities does not quite capture all there is to say about our dual loyalties. In Romans 13, the apostle Paul famously instructs fellow Christians to "be subject to the governing authorities; for there is no authority except from God," a stance that suggests compatibility between loyalty to the state and loyalty to God, as if duty to the state might be one way to exercise religious faithfulness. Similarly, in the very same passage in 1 Peter where Hauerwas and Willimon draw inspiration for their countercultural view, Christians are advised to "conduct ourselves honorably" in public, to "honor the emperor" (that is, governing authorities), and in general to see faithful citizenship as a legitimate part of faithful Christian practice. Throughout our nation's history, Christians have regarded political activity as one way to discharge religious duty, taking civic service as an opportunity to serve other people in the pattern of Jesus, and laboring to reshape American politics in the spirit of God's intentions for the world. Complete "separation of church and state" has never been the way religion and politics have played out in the United States, despite what Christians like Hauerwas and Willimon or equally strident secularists say to try and convince us this is true.[4]

If the too-easy collapse of religion into politics as suggested by the idea of a Christian America is wrong, but the radical separation of religious and political identity is also wrong—if both are bad theology and bad American history—what else can we say? How should Christians understand themselves as simultaneously Christians and Americans? I think we can say a number of things about the proper relationship between our loyalty to country and our loyalty to God, things that others in the Christian tradition

---

3. Hauerwas and Willimon, *Resident Aliens*.

4. For more on the oversimplification of "separation of church and state" as a reflection of religion and politics in US history, see my *In Defense of Civility*, ch. 3.

before us have affirmed, convictions that may help us navigate a time in which it is complicated to be simultaneously Christian and American. The most basic affirmation we can make from both a religious and a political point of view is that the nation and its government are good. President Ronald Reagan infected us forty years ago with what has become a dangerous American axiom, teaching a generation of us—Republicans and Democrats—to assume that government is not the solution to our problems, it *is* the problem.

But the demonization of national government is a hard fit for Christian tradition. From a Christian perspective, government is good, a gift of divine grace, an instrument through which human societies ensure justice, maintain order, and create conditions that allow all members of society to flourish. The medieval theologian Thomas Aquinas insisted that, as social beings, it is natural that we live in societies, but societies need government to ensure the common good:

> It is necessary that there exist among men [*sic*] some means by which the group may be governed. For where there are many men together and each one is looking after his own interest, the multitude would be broken up and scattered unless there were also an agency to take care of what appertains to the commonweal.[5]

Protestant Reformer John Calvin agreed, insisting government is necessary for the well-being of a society. In fact, he argued, government is an essential gift, and its "function among men [*sic*] is no less than that of bread, water, sun, and air; indeed, its place of honor is far more excellent."[6]

From a Christian point of view, government is not just a necessary evil that we need to keep people in line. The nation and its government are positive goods, a gift of God, something for which to be grateful. Indeed, there is nothing wrong with Christians being loyal to their nation and active in its government. Christians can embrace citizenship and even political service as commitments to the common good and laudable expressions of religious faithfulness. Being committed to our nation and the people in it can be an exercise of that great Christian principle: love thy neighbor as thyself.

5. Thomas Aquinas, *On Kingship*, 331.
6. Calvin, *Institutes*, 1488. I must admit that the regard for government as a "necessary evil," whose main reason for being is to restrain the more violent tendencies in human beings, does have root in the Christian tradition as well. But this largely negative assessment of government is a minority position; Thomas and Calvin are more typical in their assumption that government can serve the intentions of God and the needs of the commonwealth.

There is also nothing wrong necessarily with being proud of my country, of thinking that my homeland is one of the best expressions—if not *the* best expression—of justice and goodness in the world. These days that is not an assertion I am personally prepared to make, troubled as I am by the deterioration of American domestic politics as well as the US's current performance on the world stage. But national pride does not necessarily run afoul of loyalty to Christ, and there are times in our history in which we might be proud to say the efforts of American democracy were a faithful expression of Christian character as well. Even here the caution of Reinhold Niebuhr is apt, however, that equating "our particular brand of democracy with the ultimate values of life" is "a sin to which Americans are particularly prone."[7] National pride, even if justified, must always come with a healthy dose of humility if it is to be compatible with allegiance to Christ. Respecting God's sovereignty, acknowledging human limitations and failures, a Christian-flavored patriotism must always admit that one's nation is not a *perfect* reflection of God's intentions. In fact, sometimes other nations of the world serve as God's indictment on us, sounding as the bullhorn of God's judgment on a country that presumes to be a "city on a hill."

And when we are confronted with the failures of our beloved country (great and small), Christian faith and love of country demand from us prophetic protest and righteous dissent. When we are convinced US policies fail moral principle or our leaders bedevil us with decidedly immoral character, when we sense conflict between what we as Christians know is right and good and what the earthly powers of our nation ask us to accept as normal or endorse as proper, we are called as Christians to stand for what theological principle tells us is true. When God and Caesar ask different things of us, we are called to remember that we belong first and foremost to God.

When the Pharisees presented a coin to Jesus and asked him the question about taxes (Matt 22), trying to trick him into saying something religiously blasphemous or politically questionable, his answer was cleverer and more truthful than the question posed. Give to Caesar what is Caesar's, and to God what is God's, he said. But what appeared as an equivocation was instead an affirmation of the conviction that *everything* is God's! *We* belong to God! So we give to Caesar our loyalty, but first and foremost we live out our loyalty to God. We give to Caesar our loyalty, but we shade that patriotism with the colors of God's truth, whether through voting our convictions, serving in public office with integrity, exercising our right of conscience to object to immoral laws, or engaging in prophetic protest of unjust policies. When what the nation asks and what faith demands align, we serve our

---

7. Niebuhr, "Democracy as a False Religion," 257.

country with love and loyalty. When Caesar and God ask different things of us, however, we must remember we belong first and foremost to God.

To collapse being Christian and being American or to treat them as necessarily in conflict both oversimplify our duties to God and country. Give to Caesar what is Caesar's; honor the emperor; be subject to governing authorities. Be proud to be an American. Exuberant patriotism can be an expression of Christian faithfulness too. But we are called ultimately to be "a chosen race, a royal priesthood, a holy nation, God's own people" (1 Pet 2:9), set apart but set in the world to testify to the ambitious and inclusive love of the God we serve. Sometimes our commitment to the love of God in Jesus Christ underwrites our patriotism, but sometimes our Christian convictions compel us to live as "aliens and exiles" (1 Pet 2:11), in critical opposition to the politics or culture around us. Figuring out when Christian faithfulness and patriotism flow in the same direction and when they pull against each other requires more than a little bit of wisdom and discernment, but it is a responsibility to which we are all called.

These are strange times in the United States of America. For many of us, they are not confidence-inspiring, yet let us celebrate the grace-filled gift of the United States of America, whose freedoms, opportunities, and bounties give so many of us blessing upon blessing. Then may this same gratitude for the blessings of our nation inspire us to look for moments when we may bless her in return, when our commitments to God and Caesar make us vocal critics of our beloved nation, in the hope that she will be better for it.

12

Good Work

(Labor Day)

I grew up in a small coal town in western Pennsylvania. For many years, Colver was a typical company town, carved out of farm hills and physically arranged to distinguish the social status between races and ethnicities—British Isles descendants in the center of town, Eastern European enclaves at the northern and southern edges, with Jews and African-Americans pushed to the outside of town altogether. The town reflected the power differential between miners and managers, and it reinforced mining families' total dependence on the company for both income and services on which to spend their paychecks. At one time, the local theater, the store, the houses, and every utility were owned by the company. Even the name of the town reminded its citizens of company dominance, deriving as it did from a mash-up of the owners' names: Coleman and Weaver.

In its early history, Colver was an homage to coal baron power, but by the time my father returned to his hometown to work in the mines, the industry's influence over the town and surrounding area was mitigated by another force, the labor union. Once free as "job creators" to dictate the work conditions and living arrangements of their employees, coal companies increasingly had to negotiate with the collective power of the United Mine Workers of America (UMWA). As a result, the town and its residents were emancipated from singular company control. The store was privatized, competing commercial ventures were permitted, wages and benefits increased, streets were integrated (somewhat), and residents eventually won the right to own and improve the houses they lived in.

By the middle of the twentieth century, unions were an integral part of coal-town life, and my father remained active in UMWA District 2, Local 860 well after a back injury ended his active employment. Dad served as secretary of his local, and his disappearance to attend union meetings on select Sunday afternoons became a regular part of our family life, as did the presence of his binder full of minutes sitting on the living room shelves. The heavy embossing stamp sat there, too, with its readiness to make everything official, and from time to time I would sneak downstairs to give my make-believe paperwork the legitimacy of the union imprimatur. UMWA magazines appeared in the mail, filled with gripping black-and-white photographs of dirty and exhausted miners, testifying to the union's advocacy on behalf of its workers, and giving me a glimpse of the hardness that cost my father and both grandfathers their health. The UMWA ball cap that dad wore proclaimed his loyalty to the union, and when I got my own it proudly let everyone know I belonged to him.

Dad hurt his back in the mines when I was seven, but by the early eighties the rest of his fellow miners found themselves unemployed as well, displaced by the end of workable coal strips underneath our sleepy town. The coal industry remains the centerpiece of Colver's history, but by the time I became a teenager, the mine's demise (and the absence of any substitutable prospect of work) was the defining reality of the present. Union life made an impression on me, though, even if it would be years before I realized its importance beyond identity marking. As a child I heard whispers of strikes and negotiations that made very little sense to me at the time, but I would come to understand that unions were responsible for the disability compensation that allowed my parents to raise five children in strained socioeconomic circumstances. In college, I would learn the history of labor organizing in the United States, discovering raw accounts of the brutalizing working conditions in coal mines, steel mills, and factories at the beginning of the twentieth century, and the ways wealthy industry owners conspired for decades with government leaders to violently suppress efforts to organize workers. In college, I learned of the considerable cultural resistance to labor unions in the US in the first half of the last century, a fear rooted in labor movements' alleged resemblance to communist uprisings setting Europe on fire at the time. Labor eventually would prevail in its struggle for national sentiment, and aided by the friendly policies of FDR's New Deal, efforts to organize the American worker would yield employment protections we now take for granted: a minimum wage, the forty-hour work week, prohibitions on child labor, overtime compensation, health benefits, disability protections, and others.

At the turn of the twentieth century, some Christians recognized that commitment to the biblical norms of justice required the church to be actively on the side of the American worker. In a movement called the Social Gospel, Christian leaders denounced the church's apathy toward the intolerable conditions many in the working class suffered, and they called the church to focus its preaching and service on the alleviation of suffering in this life, not just the salvation of souls for the next. Reacting to massive industrialization around coal, steel, and manufacturing, the Social Gospel demanded just wages, safe working conditions, and a work week that provided adequate time for rest, religion, and family. Responding to droves descending on urban centers in search of work, the Social Gospel insisted on fair housing laws and decent living conditions for the nation's workers. Coming of age during heavy waves of immigration, the Social Gospel responded with a robust defense of new Americans' dignity and rights. To participants in this progressive Christian movement, allegiance to Jesus required the church to stand in solidarity with the suffering American worker, because Christ himself befriended the poor and oppressed.

No spokesperson for the Social Gospel was more popular than Walter Rauschenbusch, a Baptist minister and seminary professor who cut his teeth on social issues as a pastor in the Hell's Kitchen district of New York City. Profoundly affected by his parishioners' poverty and despicable working conditions, he began to see the ills of unfettered capitalism as antithetical to the moral teachings of Christianity. In an era when Christian religion was commonly thought to be concerned only with "saving souls," Rauschenbusch argued the true heart of Christianity was the prophets' vision of a just society. "The prophets," wrote Rauschenbusch, "were the heralds of the fundamental truth that religion and ethics are inseparable, and that ethical conduct is the supreme and sufficient religious act."[1] By "ethical conduct" Rauschenbusch meant "not the private morality of detached pious souls but the social morality of the nation," a social ethic based fundamentally in the prophets' solidarity with the poor.[2] The Hebrew prophets called society to be transformed into a community of justice and peace, and Jesus stood within this prophetic tradition, with a message of "social hope" symbolized by the kingdom of God. Jesus invited followers to seek the kingdom of God not as "a matter of getting individuals to heaven, but of transforming the

1. Rauschenbusch, *Christianity and the Social Crisis*, 6.
2. Rauschenbusch, *Christianity and the Social Crisis*, 8.

life on earth into the harmony of heaven."[3] According to Rauschenbusch, Jesus did not preach an escapist, otherworldly hope that ignored the ills of "a society resting on coercion, exploitation, and inequality," but instead invited those who would follow him to "found a society resting on love, service, and equality."[4]

In 1907, Rauschenbusch published *Christianity and the Social Crisis*, a blockbuster Christian interpretation of the social injustices of industrialized America. His "social Christianity" insisted the convictions of religion were incompatible with gross economic inequality, abuse of the American worker, threats to the well-being of the nation's families, and a politics in which democratic principles are overwhelmed by the power of wealth. He called on churches to preach social Christianity in their pulpits, advocate publicly for the labor class, and support legal improvements for workers, including protection of the right to organize and strike. All his prescriptions were rooted in his belief that the true heart of Christianity was not private piety but the prophetic vision of a peaceable and just human society, Christ's pronouncement of the kingdom of God on earth. Social Christianity was in an ideological battle for the soul of America, Rauschenbusch believed, for unbridled capitalism was built on "principles antagonistic to the ethics of Christianity," and if the church did not use its moral influence to mitigate capitalism's excesses, the principles of cutthroat acquisition would win. "If the Church cannot conquer business, business will conquer the Church," he said.[5]

Rauschenbusch would become the most prominent public advocate for "social Christianity" in early-twentieth-century America, something of a movement leader and public celebrity, and for a while *Christianity and the Social Crisis* would outsell every book but the Bible.[6] The Social Gospel was not a fringe leftist movement but the pulse of mainline Christianity in the early twentieth century. The Federal Council of Churches, the predecessor organization of the National Council of Churches and the representative of American mainline Protestantism in Washington, DC, issued a statement in 1908 that captured the spirit of the Social Gospel. Responding to the unregulated conditions of industrialism, "The Social Creed of the Churches" called for the elimination of excessively dangerous working conditions (including sweatshops) and child labor. It advocated for collective bargaining for labor and for more equitable distribution of the profits of production

3. Rauschenbusch, *Christianity and the Social Crisis*, 54.
4. Rauschenbusch, *Christianity and the Social Crisis*, 57.
5. Rauschenbusch, *Christianity and the Social Crisis*, 256.
6. Dorrien, *Social Ethics in the Making*, 97–98.

between owners and workers. The Creed also declared the churches' support for a weekly day of rest, a mandatory living wage, and disability and retirement incomes. In positioning the mainline Protestant church on the side of the "toilers of America" and "those who by organized effort" advocated on their behalf, the Social Creed offered not just a "pledge of sympathy" but the declaration that labor justice was a moral and religious priority, "a cause which belongs to all who follow Christ."[7]

Because of the efforts of labor organizers and their allies in the churches, by the early 1970s, the War on Poverty, dramatically declared by Lyndon B. Johnson, was effectively won. The income gap between the wealthiest Americans and the rest of the population was the lowest it had been in a hundred years, and the power of labor unions to represent the collective interests of the American working class led to vast improvement in working conditions in American industries. Fifty years later, however, we have given back many of those hard-earned accomplishments. CEO compensation is roughly 250 times the average income of the working class.[8] Historic protections like a livable income and reasonable work week are eroded by a national minimum wage that fails to keep pace with inflation, resulting in more Americans than ever working multiple jobs just to earn enough to live, often with inadequate health benefits attached to any of the jobs they hold. Workplace discrimination against women and people of color continues, albeit in more subtle ways than in generations past. Union bargaining power is weaker than it has been in nearly a century; fewer young laborers are joining unions and fewer have the option, as the federal government has retreated from its obligation to protect the right of labor to bargain collectively. Cultural bias against labor movements also has reemerged, ingeniously stoked by politicians deferring to the power brokers in major industries. Once again, the charge of "socialism" rings out against anything

7. See Federal Council of Churches, "Social Creed of the Churches," lines 17–20. Although I feature it here because it is my tradition, American mainline Protestantism was not the only voice of the Social Gospel in the last century. American Catholicism has its own rich tradition of theological solidarity with labor, which is especially poignant since many of the laborers at risk in the twentieth century were immigrants from predominantly Catholic countries. Taking their cue from a papal encyclical titled *Rerum Novarum* (1891), Catholic thinkers like John Ryan (1869–1945) argued for the moral good in labor, the natural right to organize, and the importance of a living wage as a matter of justice. See Ryan, *Economic Justice*. Catholic contributions to the cause continued through the twentieth century, including an influential pastoral letter in which the American bishops offered a robust defense of unions as a mechanism of justice. See U.S. Conference of Catholic Bishops, *Economic Justice for All*, paras. 102–9.

8. Mishel and Wolfe, "CEO Compensation Has Grown 940% since 1978."

that appears to conflict with the American gospel of *laissez-faire* capitalism, including the American tradition of union representation.

More than a hundred years later, the prophetic witness of the Social Gospel beckons to us today, for we have returned to some of the very same conditions that it stood against in its time. On the hundredth anniversary of the 1908 creed, the National Council of Churches issued another expression of social Christianity, a statement entitled "A 21st Century Social Creed." Some of its specific recommendations are in line with the creed of a century ago, a reflection of how far we have retreated from our protection of labor in the US. In an age in which workplace benefits are again under assault, the NCC calls for the elusive living wage, access to disability and retirement funds, and the right to organize. But this modern statement moves beyond the limited prescriptions of the original creed to advocate for broader social commitments that would benefit the American worker, like educational improvements, better access to housing, anti-poverty measures, fairer tax policies, and humane immigration laws. Besides addressing industry and government leaders, the creed also appeals to the American consumer, arguing for "simpler lifestyles" and "grace over greed" to reduce the demand on the labor force. Taking a more global perspective than its predecessor, it also demands the end to human trafficking and child labor, recommends worldwide fair-trade practices, and asserts the essential connection between economic justice, international peacemaking efforts, and environmental protections. The "21st Century Social Creed" roots these appeals in a commitment to the prophetic tradition of peace and justice embodied in the Social Gospel more than a century ago.[9]

Today Christians all over the United States engage in social change in the spirit of the NCC's creed. Churches participate in boycotts of fast-food chains and other industries in order to exert pressure on unjust purchasing decisions and working conditions. Leaders like the Rev. William Barber and his Moral Mondays movement commit acts of civil disobedience to protest the dismantling of the Affordable Care Act and tax policies that unfairly benefit the wealthy.[10] Interdenominational groups demonstrate before government centers in the name of fair trade agreements, just peacemaking initiatives, and environmental protections, in the knowledge that a more stable world is also a fairer world for the global laborer.

This Labor Day, more of us Christians should make the commitment to stand in solidarity with the American worker. Labor Day is one of those national holidays that once commemorated an important dimension of the

---

9. See National Council of Churches, "21st Century Social Creed."
10. Wootson, Jr., "Rev. William Barber Builds a Moral Movement."

American experience, but more often now serves as just one more three-day excuse to indulge in hot dogs and fireworks. Labor Day ought to be an annual celebration of the American worker, an acknowledgment of the importance of the working class to the common good of the United States. With all due respect to the "job creators" to whom US economic policy is so beholden, the health of our economy and our democracy depends on labor, on both the production and the consumption of our working class.[11] Beyond an opportunity to acknowledge our indebtedness to the American worker, Labor Day (at its best) serves as a ritualistic reminder of our responsibility to our laborer-citizens. This holiday annually prompts us to renew our pledge to protect the working class, in the name of the common good.

Given our theological commitment to a just society, we Christians should be leading the renewal of that Labor Day pledge. We know what those Social Gospel activists a century ago knew, that the mainline church is one of the few places in American culture where laborers and industry leaders come together and claim common community, often in the same congregation. What better place is there than church to capture the ear of the nation's wealthy elite, appeal to a shared context of justice and kinship, and lift the needs of the American worker? What could be a better discharge of our responsibility to the Social Gospel than marshalling the prophetic power of the church to call the nation to more effective public policies that support the needs, health, and well-being of the working class, on whom the common good of the United States so deeply depends?

Justice, solidarity, and the common good are religious convictions as well as social values. Similarly, Labor Day should be not just a secular holiday but a Christian holy day as well. Labor Day is the Christian Day-of-the-Prophets, the day on which we honor the vision of God's reign bequeathed to us by those seers of the Hebrew Bible, and by the One who came to proclaim good news to the poor and release to the captives. Let's make Labor Day a festival of the Social Gospel, a day when we recite the dream of Amos as our wish for the nation: "Let justice roll down like waters, and righteousness like an ever-flowing stream" (Amos 5:24).

11. Reich, *Aftershock*.

13

Fools for God

(First Day of School)

"The message about the cross is foolishness to those who are perishing," says the apostle Paul, "but to us who are being saved it is the power of God" (1 Cor 1:18). I grew up in the Rust Belt, in the mountains of southwestern Pennsylvania. I went to school for a decade in Virginia and preached in a number of small country churches around Richmond and Charlottesville. In many of the churches I knew in those places, folks embraced the foolishness of the cross as an endorsement of simple living. They wore it as a badge of honor, along with its apparent judgment of high intellectual culture's contempt for religion. For some of them, the foolishness of the cross was a defiant rejection of college-educated presumptions of superiority, specifically of scientific skepticism of biblical authority.

When I was finishing up seminary and making plans to continue my study in a PhD program, my own grandmother gave voice to this perspective. From the time I was five, Nannie was deeply invested in me becoming her "little preacher," and she became increasingly frustrated with the time I was wasting in school. "Oh, why do you need to do all that schooling," she said more than once. "I wish you could just get on with it." From her perspective, book learning was not necessarily a virtue, for the good ministers were those who just "preach the Bible" without dilution by things like the modern historical-critical methods of biblical interpretation taught in most seminaries today. Education was at best a distraction from the simple truth the Bible tells us, and at worst a threat to it.

With due respect to my beloved Nannie, I doubt that the apostle Paul meant to strike an anti-intellectual note when he called the message of the cross "foolishness." Paul was no anti-intellectual. He himself was a very intelligent man. He was highly educated in the Jewish tradition, a man of letters who invoked wisdom and literature and Hellenistic culture to convey the meaning of the gospel he felt called to preach. The theological tradition that he spurred also is one of considerable intellectual depth. Many of the so-called church fathers employed philosophical concepts to elaborate on the meanings of Jesus' life, death, and resurrection. They wrote treatises so complex, so subtle, and so conceptually deep that they remain worthy intellectual adversaries to bearers of PhDs today. Beyond religion, they had profound effect on the evolution of Western intellectual, political, and moral culture. Thinkers like Augustine, Thomas Aquinas, and Martin Luther King Jr. helped to shape how we think about war and virtue and justice, among many other things.

Many traditional Christians remain convinced, however, that intellectual culture is a distraction from the simple truth of the gospel. Just as disturbingly, their ideological opponents agree. For many critics of religion, faith necessarily requires a denial of what is real in favor of the superstitious and fantastical, making it incompatible with modern rationality. Religion's skeptics regard belief in God as a relic of earlier stages of human evolution, one that needs to disappear (or at least radically demythologize) in order for humanity to catch up to the twenty-first century. If there is need for religion at all in our time, it ought to focus on morality instead of concerning itself with the postulation of some supernatural deity. The resources of modern science and historical investigation should be allowed to prune reliance on Bible and tradition, dispensing with those archaic superstitions so that all that remains of religion is the celebration of the human project.

Some of these critics of traditional religion reside in the church. For years, Episcopal bishop John Shelby Spong has preached the message that Christianity must "change or die." The change he has in mind is the radical elimination of as much of traditional orthodoxy as possible. Doctrines like the Trinity and belief in resurrection are outdated relics from a more primitive time. Christianity must transform itself into a more rational religion suitable for the modern mind, or it will cease to be relevant to our world.[1]

1. See, for instance, Spong, *Unbelievable*. Much of Spong's message is a repeat of the "greatest hits" of more than a century of Christian liberalism, though Spong himself seems largely unaware of that liberal tradition. Dorrien wonders if Spong's unfamiliarity

Now the concern about survivability would come as a surprise to adherents beyond the US, where Christianity is not only off life support but flourishing. In fact, given traditional orthodoxy's prevalence in predominantly non-white countries and as a component of the rich heritage of the Black church in the United States, categorical diatribes against the allegedly irrational nature of traditional Christianity could be open to the charge that they are racist in their assumption of the intellectual superiority of what often looks like a white European approach to religion. In the US and Europe, though, some Christian thinkers insist religion will die if it does not revise itself in light of modern rational discourse.

Of course, many of religion's cultured despisers would prefer it not survive at all. The scientist Richard Dawkins has been perhaps the most vocal of critics, writing books in the name of a "New Atheism," in which he asserts that belief in God is delusional and leads to infantile moral judgment. Religion is a dangerous fantasy, Dawkins insists, and those who think they can be religious and intelligent at the same time are fooling themselves. And lest you think Dawkins has only Christian fundamentalists in mind, he makes clear his disdain for allegedly progressive religion, too; those of us who would identify as progressive Christians just enable the more dangerous kind, he says.[2]

What both Christian anti-intellectualism and the hyper-modern critic share is a fundamentalist approach to questions of religion. They see the world in zealous binary terms. You can be either this or that, either rational or religious, but you cannot be both. Either you subscribe to Scripture or to the data of modern science, but you cannot meaningfully do both. Faith and reason are opposites, they tell us. In the company of either, be careful of what you choose. The anti-intellectual Christian will tell you that if you choose to embrace modern history and science, if you believe in evolution or suggest that Moses may not have written the first five books of the Bible (books that depict his own death!) or concede that the Gospels may not be rock-solid historical biography, then you are not a real Christian. The hyper-modern critic will insist that if you take seriously the insights of tradition, if you fail to laugh out loud at stories of miracles or if you betray a fondness for old

---

with the deeper tradition of Christian liberalism may have been a consequence of his Episcopal Church's limited role in that tradition, as well as the limited exposure he probably had while living and working in the American South, where liberalism had less of a foothold. As a result, Dorrien amusingly notes, "Spong often gave the impression that liberal theology began with his books" (Dorrien, *Making of American Liberal Theology*, 3:528).

2. Dawkins, *God Delusion*.

doctrinal formulas and ancient myths, then you cannot be reasonable. One camp calls your faith into question, the other challenges your intelligence.

Now at the risk of arrogance, I will admit I consider myself a pretty smart guy who also cherishes much of Christian history and tradition, but according to these two camps, that just means I am screwed no matter which way I go. To be frank, I find both camps obviously deficient in understanding, frequently infuriating, and equally fundamentalist in tone. They both offer pithy litmus tests for "right" thinking, and if you disagree with them then you are either faithless or an idiot. They are, in fact, fundamentalist mirror images of each other, for they both subscribe to the erroneous assumption that faith and reason are opposites.

In reality, the vast majority of the Christian tradition has reflected some version of the conviction that wisdom is a *unifying* thesis between faith and reason. It is no accident that many of the great thinkers in the history of Christian thought also represent pinnacles in Western intellectual history. St. Augustine, the most important Christian theologian short of Jesus and Paul, was also an architect of political realism and the just war tradition. Thomas Aquinas, the father of Catholic theology, built his theology as much on the Aristotelian philosophy he helped recover for Western culture as he did the Bible. Jonathan Edwards, that early American Calvinist unfortunately better known for the sermon "Sinners in the Hand of an Angry God," was in fact one of the most important philosophical minds in American history. He was deeply informed by Enlightenment thought and so much in the vanguard of scientific literacy that he volunteered for small-pox inoculation—an unfortunate decision, perhaps, because it killed him.

Reinhold Niebuhr was not only one of the most important theologians of the last century, but he was a first-rate political thinker who profoundly affected American economic and foreign policy from the 1930s to today; former President Obama cited him frequently as a major influence. Martin Luther King Jr. was a once-in-a-generation public intellectual who moved masses toward his dream for a just society by weaving biblical allusions into his invocations of American democratic principles. Up until her death a few years ago, Jean Bethke Elshtain was a nationally known political philosopher at the University of Chicago who celebrated unapologetically the influence of Christian intellectual heritage on her understanding of political responsibility.

These are just a few of the examples of the marriage of faith and reason in the Christian tradition. *Anyone who subscribes to a historic antithesis between Christian faith and reason does not know this tradition.* So whatever the "foolishness" of the gospel meant to Paul, it seems unlikely that it meant a rejection of intelligence and wisdom. The Christian message is not anti-intellectual, despite being packaged that way from time to time in modern churches. Christianity does not celebrate anti-intellectualism, and neither should we. I think Americans in particular have done enough of that lately, to deleterious effect.

But if the foolishness of the gospel Paul refers to is not a rejection of intelligence and learning, then what is it? Why does he characterize the gospel as foolishness in the eyes of those who do not believe? Paul insists it is the "message of the cross" that is foolishness to the world that will not subscribe to it. What appears as idiocy is the idea of a religious and moral worldview with crucifixion at its center. That is the foolishness. That is what the world does not know how to handle.

Truth be told, a lot of times neither do we. We Christians are much too prone to displace the cross, ignore it, or sanitize it in our embrace of Christian belief. On the conservative side of the faith, we turn it into an escape pod from this life that otherwise has no apparent effect on the choices we make in this life. Jesus died for me on the cross, and therefore I am saved, no matter what I do. On the liberal side, we try really hard to pretend that the cross is not there at all. We prefer to focus on the aphorisms of Jesus and his model of a morally respectable life. His death becomes an unfortunate historical development, rather than an event with any kind of theological significance.

Yet Paul insists the message of the cross *is* the gospel of Christ. The apex of Jesus' mission and ministry was not the Sermon on the Mount but his death between thieves. That is certainly how each of the Gospels tells his story as well. The message of the cross is the gospel of Jesus Christ. Paul makes clear that ultimately the gospel of the cross strikes many in the world as foolishness because it is a countercultural set of priorities. It is not commentary on intelligence or education but an assertion of *values* that run counter to the ones the world often celebrates. At the center of the church's founding story is an execution and the humiliation, suffering, isolation, and powerlessness that comes with such an ignominious act. And yet, says our sacred story, there is where we shall find God. The message of the cross is that in that occasion of tragedy and injustice and humility, we shall find the steadfastness of God.

The message of the cross is more radical than what passes for conventional wisdom. The cross declares that God is the one waiting for us in our tragedies. It assures us God is on the side of the poor, the outcast, the despised, and all those who have not won the social lottery. The message of the cross declares that the Source of all that is good can be found especially among those whom society loathes or mistrusts, or who are told they are no longer welcome. It insists that in the most horrific brutality that human beings can unleash on one another, God is present, renders a judgment on that brutality, and ultimately reigns victorious over it.

As theologian James Cone puts it, "The cross is a paradoxical religious symbol because it *inverts* the world's value system with the news that hope comes by way of defeat, that suffering and death do not have the last word, that the last shall be first and the first last."[3] The message of the cross is countercultural wisdom because it swims against the tide of dominant values in our world and in fact indicts them. Paul himself puts it this way:

> But God chose what is foolish in the world to shame the wise;
> God chose what is weak in the world to shame the strong; God
> chose what is low and despised in the world, things that are not,
> to reduce to nothing things that are, so that no one might boast
> in the presence of God. (1 Cor 1:27–29)

The foolishness of God insists that transactional savvy—deal-making—is not wisdom, because wisdom is relational and moral. The foolish wisdom of God builds bridges instead of burning them, and it cultivates community rather than dividing houses. The foolish wisdom of God insists that real strength is not found in intimidation or will to power, but in service, sacrifice, sharing, building others up, and preserving the dignity and integrity of all people. The foolish wisdom of the cross declares that blessing comes not through self-serving prosperity but through generosity, not from taking care of ourselves first, but by sacrificing and serving others and the common good, as inclusively as we can define it. According to the wisdom of the cross, the true expression of our humanity is not competition but community. Ultimately we are not of Paul or of Cephas, not conservative or liberal, insiders or outsiders, Republican or Democrat, Americans or foreigners. The truest expression of our humanity comes when we are united in the same mind and purpose. Who is the greatest among us? He who identifies with the least among us, says the One who went to the cross. Greatness is not defined by winning but by losing ourselves that others might gain and God might be glorified.

In the cross's value system, success is defined not by pointing to oneself but by gesturing to others. Success is measurable when people have hope, when they are cured of their disease and protected from their sickness, when they can see light in the darkness and kinship in one another again. God's foolishness stands worldly values on their head and defines success against the kingdom of God, where people will come from east and west and

---

3. Cone, *Cross and the Lynching Tree*, 2; italics original.

from north and south and sit together with the Christ who signaled God's truth with arms wide open on, of all things, a cross.

Christian faith is not incompatible with the best of human knowledge. What Christian faith brings to the table is a view of the bigger picture, a larger context of values in which to understand, embrace, utilize, and critique all of the other sources of knowledge at our disposal. Christian wisdom understands the project of being human with a wide-angle moral lens. We understand that we exist in and for a world that is not our own, a world of gift and grace, a world on which we depend and that depends upon us. We understand ourselves to live under the divine canopy, and we derive a sense of responsibility from that realization.

From this enlarged perspective, then, the "foolish" Christian celebrates the richness of human intellect and industry, while remaining critical of the excesses that threaten those with whom we share God's canopy. The foolish Christian embraces science as a good gift, while remaining respectful of mystery and wary of the so-called scientific imperative and its pressure to equate what we *can* do technologically with what we *must* do. The foolish Christian embraces economic and political philosophy, while reserving the right to call out ideologues who elevate concepts like "wealth," "capitalism," and even "democracy" to uncontestable goods. Christian wisdom is intelligence with the benefit of a wide-angle lens.

When friends or foes of Christianity, therefore, try to convince you that this religion is anti-intellectual, do not believe them! Christianity is the love of wisdom, with a twist. It is the pursuit of wisdom in service to an ethic of the cross. The inclusive love and irrepressible hope the cross symbolizes energize our pursuit of learning and our gratitude for the life of the mind. Christianity affirms the life of wisdom and learning, but our attention to the message of the cross makes us look like fools to those who define smarts without a corresponding obligation to serve God and others with our intellectual gifts. We can deal with their dismissal, though, for we are lovers of true wisdom and fools for Christ, and the foolishness of God's reign is what helps us endure the fools we encounter in this one.

14

Though this World with Devils Filled

(Halloween)

The televangelist Pat Robertson has called Halloween "the day when millions of children and adults will be dressing up as devils, witches, and goblins . . . to celebrate Satan."[1] According to Robertson, we give our children over to the adoration of the devil when we allow them to masquerade about town as zombies and ghouls, for Halloween has its roots in pagan worship. Robertson seems unaware that Halloween has at least as many roots in the Christian calendar, in the observance of All Souls' Day, a ritualistic commemoration of the dead that accompanies the holy day of All Saints. Then again, Robertson was the television preacher who told my generation that the Saturday morning cartoon *The Smurfs* also encouraged Satan worship because it featured witchcraft and magic. I have little doubt that annoying TV show was a gift of the devil, but not because it featured witches—just because anything that mind-numbingly stupid must originate in hell.

I confess I do not fear for the souls of my children or their friends because they like to dress up as something scary and extort candy from

1. Quoted in Holley, "Pat Robertson Says." According to Holley, nearly two in five Americans (mostly evangelicals) share some version of Robertson's view of the holiday.

neighbors. Our world hosts too many real demons already to worry about the ones that come out on Halloween. As I sit here in the fall of 2019, we face the mortgaging of our ecological future to big oil and big coal. We have grown numb to record-breaking degrees of inequality between the wealthiest 1 percent of Americans and the rest of us. We suffer through a dysfunctional national government and a president with little respect for the rule of law. We face a persistent failure of leadership when the need for reasonable gun control is raised, while frequent mass shootings (often in our schools) put us all at risk, and most Americans—even gun owners like me—recognize the need for more sensible and effective laws. No, the effect of Halloween on our children does not concern me, Pat. There are too many real devils at work in the world; I cannot get riled up about the make-believe kind.

Because those real demons terrorize us, I think we American Protestants would be well served to focus our energies on the *other* holiday that comes around at the end of October: Reformation Sunday. Some 500 years ago, on October 31, 1517, Martin Luther is said to have reached his limit in his frustration over abusive practices in the Roman Church. He nailed his ninety-five theses (or points of contention) to the church door in Wittenberg, prompting the public debate that eventually would lead to his break from the Roman Church and the birth of Protestant Christianity. The Reformation was a game-changer in the church, remaking the face of global Christianity, but beyond the church it effected a cultural revolution too. The Reformation transformed art and music by spurring the development of secular traditions of aesthetic expression. It cultivated German national identity and literacy by contributing to the maturation of German language. It led to a revolution in science by helping to usher Europe into the modern period of knowledge acquisition. It led to a revolution in politics by contributing to the emergence of democratic principles, freedom of conscience, and human rights.

The Reformation was a revolutionary force, not just for religion but for many other aspects of human culture and society, and perhaps recapturing the spirit of the Reformation is the catalyst we so desperately need in our time. In this mire of injustice, incivility, and mutual suspicion in which we find ourselves, faced with the dual temptations of aggressive tribalism or cynical paralysis, we need a reformation of the American character. The church can help lead that reform, but to do so we must mobilize around a couple of enduring truths we inherited from that great Reformation 500 years ago.

The first Reformation truth I think we must embrace is a realistic assessment of our predicament. Things are as bad as they seem right now, and it is not as simple as a limited number of bad people doing bad things. We suffer not just from individual leaders behaving badly, but from the perversity of a political process that gives irresponsibility power and rewards the abandonment of duty and principle. The appearance of white nationalists on the streets of Charlottesville and the revelation of Hollywood moguls abusing women are not simply instances of a couple of bad actors, but symptoms of a diseased society that provides fertile ground for the perpetuation of racial hatred and misogyny. Our problem is not just a few politicians who are hostile to the idea of basic health insurance, but a culture that allows us to grow numb to the reality that millions of people lack adequate access to good health care, enough that it threatens their physical and economic survival. We languish not just because of stunningly egoistic leadership in Washington, but because that leadership has seduced us into abandoning any principled commitment to the common good, training us to ask instead, "what are those people [read: women, people of color, immigrants, gay people, the poor] getting over on me?"

Things are as bad as they seem right now, so much so that the classical Calvinist term *depravity* seems apt, for we are confronting not just specific people behaving badly but an unhealthy ethos in which we are all complicit. John Calvin described the human condition as sin, "vitiated and perverted" by pride, ambition, and other modes of inordinate self-concern. He insisted this condition ran deep in human beings, and "continually bears new fruits . . . just as a burning furnace gives forth flame and sparks, or water ceaselessly bubbles up from a spring."[2] Although the term *sin* makes some of us of a liberal stripe cringe, I still find it helpful as an indication of the depth to the challenges that lie before us. Without the language of sin, I fear we underestimate the moral work we have to do.

Calvin insisted sin is more than an individual failing, and "it is falsely said . . . that man [*sic*] sins out of ignorance alone," for often we share general moral principles only to misapply them conveniently to ourselves. For example, he said, "every man will affirm that murder is evil. But he who is plotting the death of an enemy contemplates murder as something good. The adulterer will condemn adultery in general, but will privately flatter himself in his own adultery."[3] Perhaps more to our circumstances, "every man" will reject big government safety nets, until it is his turn to cash his unemployment or Social Security check. "Every man" decries the negative effects of immigration, while conveniently ignoring the benefits of gracious immigration policy on his own family's story.

2. Calvin, *Institutes*, 251.
3. Calvin, *Institutes*, 282.

The theological language of sin reminds us we are dealing with a pervasive ethos of self-absorption that sometimes gets the best of us and our commitment to the common good. That is why I think we Christians ought to intentionally embrace this Reformation concept and utilize it in our current social critique, despite liberal squeamishness over the term. Writing in the last century, Protestant theologian and public intellectual Reinhold Niebuhr charged liberalism with dismissing the seriousness of sin, leading them to a naïve assessment of cultural conflict:

> They [Christian liberals] regard social conflict either as an impossible method of achieving morally approved ends or as a momentary expedient which a more perfect education or a purer religion will make unnecessary. They do not see that the limitations of the human imagination, the easy subservience of reason to prejudice and passion, and the consequent persistence of irrational egoism, particularly in group behavior, make social conflict an inevitability in human history, probably to its very end.[4]

Excessively optimistic about the potential of reason and feelings of kinship, Christian liberals often downplay the language of sin as archaic and oppressive. They speak as if people can just educate, love, or hug away the things that divide them. Niebuhr, however, was convinced our national and global problems are more deeply rooted in the human condition than a reliance on reason or affection alone might address. Human conflict, he said, stems from our tendency to define and care for ourselves at the expense of others. It derives from a "misery," a self-absorption, that Christians historically called sin:

> The church knows, or ought to know, that though men may be incredibly stupid, the hatred and contempt that they exhibit in their lives springs from a deeper source than stupidity. It is the consequence of the corruption of a greater spiritual freedom in man than those understand who speak of man as "rational." Both the dignity and the misery of man are greater than modern culture understands. The misery of man is derived from his idolatry, from his partly conscious and partly unconscious effort to make himself, his race, and his culture God.[5]

The "misery" that drives us to define ourselves as the pinnacle of good at the expense of others resides not just in the hearts of people but in the

---

4. Niebuhr, *Moral Man and Immoral Society*, xx.
5. Niebuhr, "Christian Faith and the Race Problem," 129.

structures, institutions, and movements of society, and it leads to the entrenched anger, fear, mutual suspicion, conflict, and violence that plague our social lives together.

I am convinced some of the liberal bewilderment over events in this country since 2016 is explained by our abandonment of the language of sin. How else can racism be so alive and well in this country, not just in individual hearts but entrenched in institutional practices? How can so many people continually vote against their economic self-interests, for politicians who promise to advocate for them but fill their own pockets at their constituents' expense? How have we dispensed so thoroughly with the intellectual and moral qualifications for leadership? How did so many Christian evangelicals resolve the obvious disconnect between their presidential choices and the sense of biblical morality they praise in their churches? Our social challenges are not adequately captured by charges of mere ignorance. They betray something fundamentally amiss in the human condition. Things are as bad as they seem, and they defy easy explanation. We are seeing the dark shadows of the human condition, the complexities of sin.

Reformation theology takes this human condition seriously, but then it insists there is more to the story. Onto the stage of human sin enters the triumphant power of grace. Grace is the second Reformation conviction we ought to hold up in our moment, the rallying cry of the cultural revolution we seek to inspire. Grace is the belief in radical forbearance and enduring patience, the extension of love in the name of the One who first loved us. Grace is the promise my home congregation declares every Sunday, when we recite as a countercultural witness that "no matter who you are or where you are on life's journey, you are welcome here," because God welcomes all of us.

Grace is in short supply these days. Without grace, we assume there are conditions to whether others are welcome. Do you look like me? Were you born here? Do you vote with my political party? Do you own guns? Do you have a job? Without grace, we assume other people's worth is conditional and measurable, and it easily evaporates.

In a world without grace, you are your apparent transgressions. Did you vote for Donald Trump? Then you are a racist, says the other side. Do you believe in abortion rights for women? Then you are complicit in the murder of children and have no regard for the sanctity of human life, says the other side. Did you once utter something that we now recognize as racist, misogynist, homophobic, or otherwise hurtful? Then you shall be shunned, and there is no room for do-overs, no opportunity for apologies, no appetite for narratives of maturation. The phenomenon of "cancel culture," where celebrities and regular folks alike are boycotted for saying or doing something offensive, strikes me as a predictable development in a world of instant communication and no grace. In cancel culture, you are your mistake or shortsightedness, and there is little patience for constructive engagement and critique, never mind forgiveness and growth. Without grace, there is no middle ground. By contrast, grace reminds us that mistakes are inevitable, life is complicated, and we never know for sure whether we are completely on the side of what is right or good, so healthy doses of forgiveness and patience and the benefits of doubt are warranted in the disagreements in which we find ourselves.

We need a lot more grace in the world, the reminder that we are more than our failings or missteps. We need to hear that we matter, that all people deserve dignity, respect, justice, inclusion, and patience, for the simple reason that we are all human beings, children of God. The value that comes from grace allows us to love ourselves, and it empowers us to love others, even when we do not particularly like what they do or stand for. Grace also gives us hope, because if our transgressions are not all there is to say about us, if God's grace gives us a dignity and worth and potential that extends beyond the badness, then that grace also promises the power to improve the badness in and around us. Without trust in the power of grace, we have no reason to expect anything beyond what we currently see in people, systems, politics, or institutions. Without trust in the power of grace, we are left with cynicism, self- or other-loathing, and paralysis. Grace gives us hope, even when the justifying evidence for that hope appears thin.

Armed with that hope, we are free to embrace the third Reformation conviction that can empower revolution in our time and place: the holy priesthood. Martin Luther rejected a medieval theology that mandated an intermediary to access God. Instead Luther insisted we *all* are priests. We all have direct access to God's love. We are all immediate beneficiaries of grace, and as a result, we are all direct conduits of grace. The church is not an institution that dispenses grace as a scarce commodity, but a community of people who channel grace in obnoxious surplus.

In the face of entrenched injustice, we the church model something else, a sanctuary of inclusion, friendship, and basic human respect. In the midst of obscene divisiveness, we practice radical loving community. In an ethos of mutual suspicion, we assume the best in one another, welcome strangers, embrace difference, and practice forbearance. With due respect for Calvin and Niebuhr's reminder of the reality of sin, we reject cynicism and instead preach a message of hope and a vision of promise. Through inclusive programming, hospitable space, moral budgets, prophetic worship, tireless advocacy, and faithful public presence, churches actively resist a culture of selfishness and violence and participate in an insurgency of inclusion, solidarity, cooperation, and justice. For we are high priests of God, revolutionaries bathed in the doctrine of grace. Sin is real, but grace is more, and we are ambassadors of that message.

So take seriously the complicated destructive realities in the human condition, manifest in our own time—how can we not? But as Christians, refuse to despair. Resist the temptation to cynicism, loathing, and passivity. Instead, see this present darkness as an opportunity to exercise the duties of priesthood, to receive and to channel God's grace in a world losing touch with grace. Despite abundant evidence to the contrary, Christians insist (as MLK often said) the arc of the moral universe bends toward justice, and that grace pushes productively against hate. May God use us to lean into that shove. With confidence let us sing Luther's famous hymn: *"And though this world, with devils filled, should threaten to undo us, we will not fear, for God hath willed His truth to triumph through us."*[6] For this is precisely why we are in the world, to testify to God's goodness, and to personify it. We are built to convey hope in dark times, to embody love and community, to commend cooperation and solidarity, and ultimately to witness to a better way of being human than the devils who fill this world want us to imagine.

As the autumn leaves fall from their trees, weather itself reminds us that the reality of death always comes before the good news of resurrection. We have bigger things to worry about than whether trick-or-treating is contributing to the spiritual delinquency of our children, for the world seems to be plummeting to hell in a handbasket. But armed with tried-and-true Reformation principles, may we witness to the gospel of reconciliation and help restore some semblance of decency and justice to our common life together. Thank God for the wisdom and legacy of that Reformation 500 years ago—but the next one is ours to effect.

6. "A Mighty Fortress Is Our God" (1529), verse 3.

15

Six or Seven Things God Hates

(Election Day)

Recently I stumbled across a passage in Proverbs I do not remember ever reading before, even though I have read through my Bible cover to cover several times in my life. (It is possible I skimmed the aphorisms in Proverbs during my obligations to Sunday school!) The passage is Proverbs 6:16–19:

> There are six things that the Lord hates,
> seven that are an abomination to him:
> haughty eyes, a lying tongue,
> and hands that shed innocent blood,
> a heart that devises wicked plans,
> feet that hurry to run to evil,
> a lying witness who testifies falsely,
> and one who sows discord in a family.

According to this biblical proverb, arrogance, dishonesty, violence against the innocent, deceitfulness, destructive impulsiveness, false witness, and divisiveness are character traits that God does not just reject but abhors. God hates these vicious habits, the Bible tells us.

Given the real angst many people are feeling about the moral culture in American politics these days, I doubt I am the only one who reads this list and notices how close to home it hits. The vices listed here are all deviances that run amok in our current political climate, with presidential imprimatur. Mr. Trump is constitutionally unable to admit he is wrong, and in fact he regularly boasts he knows more than the military, medical, or economic experts around him. The legal assault on immigrants and the economic sacrifice of the working class to the desires of the 1 percent has inflicted physical hardship and emotional pain on thousands of people, including innocent children. The war on the "fake news" media and daily barrage of falsehoods have undermined our trust in fundamental institutions of our democracy, and more broadly have eviscerated the concept of truth.[1] Perhaps most insidiously, the president's considerable skill set in divisive rhetoric and political positioning have aggravated existing fissures in the American electorate, teaching us to fear one another as enemies instead of seeing each other as fellow citizens with whom we may disagree on important issues. The six or seven things God hates happen to be the parameters of "politics as usual" in this new normal in which we live.

Some years ago, I wrote a book in which I argued that religious communities and their traditions could be instrumental to cultivating the virtues of citizenship that a well-functioning democracy depends on.[2] I called those virtues "civility," and I suggested faith communities can provide Americans with the opportunity to nurture and practice traits like humility, patience, integrity, and respect, for the betterment of those faith communities and the nation. Then along came Donald Trump, and suddenly folks on the left and the right of the political spectrum were asking whether civility was even a viable aspiration for American politics. Critics of Mr. Trump argued he was eroding the standards for public discourse beyond repair and endangering the prospects for national unity. They objected to his brazen contempt for public decorum and respect, citing his tendency to ridicule women, people of color, the disabled, and anyone who disagreed with him (even within his own political party). Trump's supporters pointed to the vitriol his antagonists aimed at him and argued he was not alone in abandoning conventions of political civility, just more honest about it. After the 2016 presidential election, many Americans were left wondering if *civil* discourse and public virtue were even possible in the United States anymore.

1. As of this writing, the *Washington Post*'s Fact Checker has documented over 16,000 false statements that Donald Trump has made since becoming president. See Kessler et al., "President Trump Made 16,241 False or Misleading Claims." This tally does not include the president's misleading rhetoric around the spread of COVID-19 in the United States in early 2020, misrepresentation that seriously compromised our readiness for the pandemic.

2. See Davis, *In Defense of Civility*.

Proverbs reminds us, however, that character matters in a healthy society. Character matters to a community seeking to be and do good. The six
or seven things God considers an abomination paint a vivid picture of the
absence of public character, but the New Testament provides us several lists
of positive character, virtues that make for good community. The Letter to
the Ephesians, that primer in Christian ethics, commends humility, gentle-
ness, patience, and forbearance. The Letter to the Colossians counsels us
to put off old ways of malice and slander and practice instead compassion,
meekness, forgiveness, and love. According to the New Testament, these
virtues are signs of Christian character and healthy community. To the extent that we believe the gospel represents God's intentions for all humanity,
then these virtues represent more than just good piety for Christians in their
churches; they describe what it means to be true moral community.

Three-plus years into the Trump presidency, we can confirm that public character is now on life support. At the same time, we need to be careful
declaring that the state of our politics is the worst it has ever been. That is a
dubious claim for a nation whose history pivots on a civil war and the practice of human enslavement. American politics has always been brutal. Just
consider the personal insults between John Adams and Thomas Jefferson in
the election of 1800, the racism at work on both sides of debates over Emancipation, the social upheaval of the 1960s, or the constitutional trauma of
Watergate. Throughout US history, the idea of public virtue always has been
more aspiration than accomplishment, yet there is something distinct about
this current moment. Brazen racists have found new voice, undermining
our national myth of moral progress and deflating our hopes that we might
move beyond the penance required for America's "original sin." Conservatives abandon and liberals endlessly deconstruct any shared understanding
of "American ideals," depriving us of a standard for right and wrong beyond
self-interest, personified in a president who is happily ignorant of American principles and who governs exclusively by impulse, appetite, and self-
service. Substantive meaning of the word *truth* itself has evaporated, leaving
us unmoored and nihilistic, ill-prepared to come together in moments of
national crisis (like the coronavirus pandemic) because we no longer can
depend on facts or the trustworthiness of our leaders and experts. The idea
of an era of perfect political virtue in American history may be a fiction, but
it is also true that our moment seems especially distant from any moral ideal
for our collective national life.

The dearth of public virtue feels so bad to many Americans because
we experience it not just as a political predicament but a *moral* crisis. There
are those who tell us that morality has no place in politics. Political realists (devotees of Machiavelli and others) insist politics is solely about the

acquisition and maintenance of power, not the pursuit of virtue. Appeals to moral standards in politics are unrealistic and misplaced, the realists tell us, but in doing so they subscribe to a convenient misunderstanding of American history. In truth, our politics has always been laced with a sense of moral purpose. From its opening chapter in that Puritan effort to construct a "city on a hill," to the struggle for independence, to the wrought chaos of civil war, to a myriad of domestic conflicts and international engagements in the modern era, Americans have collectively understood their nation as one with a moral duty to the world. Obviously, this is not to say we have consistently gotten that responsibility right. The United States has often been on the wrong side of the moral universe. Our commitment to moral duty has been misshapen and compromised by the ever-present temptation to prioritize national interest over global good, as well as our penchant for justifying oppression and harboring injustice. Even in our darker chapters, though, we have strived to understand ourselves as a moral nation and to understand our political responsibilities in a moral framework. The challenges our nation faced were assumed to have moral consequence, and commitment to the ideals of the American character, however contested, served as the basic vocabulary for struggling together through war, racism, genocide, inequality, terrorism, and natural disaster.

That moral vocabulary no longer serves us. These days we lack a shared sense of the good. This is in part because we no longer have collective confidence in the ideals of our nation's "sacred texts." The Declaration of Independence and the US Constitution, charters of our nation's moral identity, have rightly been called out for the abominations they contain. Racism and sexism are baked into our foundational texts. The Declaration's celebration of life, liberty, and the pursuit of happiness falls on cynical ears, as we recognize better than ever the tragic irony in an appeal to inalienable rights from the pen of a man who owned other human beings. The Constitution was constructed for a new nation where Black men were counted as less than human, and women were not counted as political actors. Historical perspective and a couple of amendments correct for the myopia in both texts, but their imperfections tempt us to doubt their moral authority, which in turn calls into question the moral ideals they lift up as what bind Americans one to another.

We Christians of a liberal bent know a little something about the tightrope walk between honoring the ideals of your moral texts and traditions and responsibly critiquing and revising them to reflect the moral universe as we now experience it. To be a person of faith today requires me to discern the persistent truths of the Christian tradition—fundamental commitments to life, love, justice, and community—while also admitting parts of my religious heritage no longer resonate with an understanding of the world rooted in the twenty-first century. Similarly, the ideals of life and happiness, the essential balance between individual liberty and commitment to the common good—these markers of moral purpose rise above our flawed national documents and remain the moral foundation to our collective sense of self, even if they require us to reinterpret them in every new moment.

Reinterpreting the obligations of our moral ideals, in fact, is itself an American tradition. Abolitionists in the nineteenth century and suffragists in the early twentieth appealed to constitutional ideals to make the case for emancipation and political empowerment, urging the country to move past the injustice in the ways it had interpreted those same ideals in generations past. Closer to our time, Martin Luther King Jr. gave powerful voice to the continuing relevance of those historic ideals to a nation past due in its recognition of the rights of all its citizens. From the steps of the Lincoln Memorial, he preached:

> So I say to you, my friends, that even though we must face the difficulties of today and tomorrow, I still have a dream. It is a dream deeply rooted in the American dream that one day this nation will rise up and live out the true meaning of its creed— we hold these truths to be self-evident, that all men are created equal.[3]

In the inspiring crescendo of his "I Have a Dream" speech, King testified to the enduring power of American moral ideals. Mixing invocation of American virtues like brotherhood and freedom with the prophetic thunder of biblical calls for justice, King insisted our commitment to a sense of public virtue was what underwrote his hope that we could become a nation better than its past, a nation all of its citizens could consider a "sweet land of liberty." Political life in the United States always has been moral aspiration; it always has been a collective commitment to moral duty. It also is a contest between ethical perspectives, in which our memories and (to use Emilie Townes's wonderful phrase) "countermemory" of the American moral tradition, voices with power and voices without, appeal in point and counterpoint to the best in our national character, wrestling for the chance to shape the moral vector of the nation.[4]

Politics is a moral endeavor, one that places moral responsibility on all of us to craft a society that pursues what is right and good. In a republic, that in turn requires we ensure our leaders and representatives share that

3. King, "I Have a Dream," 219.
4. Townes, *Womanist Ethics and the Cultural Production of Evil*, 8.

sense of moral duty and possess the ethical character to discharge it. That makes voting a profound moral act. For Christians whose sense of moral responsibility stems from their religious worldview, it then stands to reason that voting is also an obligation of faithfulness. This is not to say we Christians should only vote for other Christians or for the institutionalization of Christianity. There are good reasons for Christians who live in a pluralistic society to respect the disestablishment of religion.[5] At the same time, we Christians should understand there are moral consequences to the choices we make as citizens, including whether to vote and for whom to vote. And insofar as our understanding of those moral consequences is rooted in our religious worldview, it gives the duties of citizenship, including voting, a faith importance as well. In a sense, Election Day is a holy day of profound religious responsibility.

There are those who will tell us religion has no place in politics, and Christianity should concern itself with the spiritual, not the political. Anyone who claims strict "separation of church and state" as a Christian ideal, however, fails to understand the gospel of Christ, for following the Way of Jesus has consequences on who we are as citizens as well as individuals. Jesus said as much in response to religious leaders who tried to trap him into uttering a false dichotomy that would risk blasphemy and sedition. They asked him, "Is it lawful to pay taxes to the emperor, or not?" To which Jesus replied, "Give to the emperor the things that are the emperor's, and to God the things that are God's" (Mark 12:13–17). The Gospel of Mark tells us Jesus' interrogators were left "amazed" by his response, and ever since this episode has been interpreted different ways within the church, but to me the story conveys the muddy middle ground from which Christians must understand their political responsibilities. On the one hand, Jesus implies there is virtue in satisfying our civic responsibilities ("Give to the emperor the things that are the emperor's"), while on the other hand, he reminds us of our obligation to give "to God the things that are God's." The logic of Christian belief reminds us that *all* things are God's, so while he affirms the good in satisfying obligations of citizenship, Jesus also creates space for us to settle conflict between our political duties and fidelity to God in favor of the latter. Christian political duty is a subset of our all-encompassing fidelity to God.[6]

5. There is a difference between voting with faith convictions as your motivation and voting specifically for the establishment of Christian priorities, but that distinction is more complicated than I can do justice to here. For a good discussion of some of the reasons Christians can theologically honor religious disestablishment in a pluralistic society like the United States, see Ronald Thiemann's *Religion in Public Life*.

6. The apostle Paul also insisted on seeing political duty through the lens of faith

In subsuming political obligation under the obligations God places on us, Christ was simply continuing the prophetic tradition in which he stood. The prophets were explicitly political actors. Their diatribes were calls for political reform, beseeching the nation-state and its leaders to return to the ideals of justice and peace to which God called all humanity. When Micah insisted God requires us "to do justice, and to love kindness, and to walk humbly with your God" (Mic 6:8), he was challenging the entire nation of Israel and its political rulers. His religious imperative had clear social consequence, for it is hard to do justice alone. Similarly, when Amos imagined justice rolling like waters (Amos 5:24), he was offering a political vision, not just a private morality. Christians who walk in the lineage of the prophets and the Way of Jesus know our political lives constitute moral obligations, governed by religious values.

If we understand the religious and moral significance of political involvement this way, then seeing Election Day through the lens of faith should motivate us to vote and shape our evaluation of candidates for leadership. Do those who desire to lead us possess the character necessary to make America morally good again? What might that character look like? The answer to those questions is easy. The character of good leadership is reflected in the One we Christians follow, who exhibited humility, prioritized peace, insisted on justice, and embodied truth. The character of good leadership promotes healthy community, as described in the Pauline virtues of patience, forbearance, compassion, cooperation, and love.[7] It decidedly does not include the six or seven things the Bible tells us God hates. Discerning the difference between those with a character consistent with Jesus and leaders who exhibit the opposite—who act, literally, as the anti-Christ—is one of the great responsibilities of public faithfulness in our time.

---

when he counseled Christians in Rome: "Let every person be subject to the governing authorities; for there is no authority except from God, and those authorities that exist have been instituted by God" (Rom 13:1). Paul reminds us that political citizenship is a Christian moral obligation because our civic commitment to one another normally is an expression of mutual regard, and mutual regard reflects our fidelity to God. At the same time, he and other apostles clearly left open the prerogative to honor God over the emperor when the demands of those two loyalties diverged, as they attested in the "political disobedience" that led to their deaths.

7. For more on this biblical tradition of virtuous living together, and how it represents an important public witness in a polarized political moment, see my *Forbearance*, especially ch. 9.

16

Thanksgiving Leftovers

(Thanksgiving Day)

Thanksgiving is a kind of high holy day for Puritan scholars like me. It is, therefore, my habit in November to pull from my shelf my worn copy of William Bradford's *Of Plymouth Plantation* and read a little bit about that first band of Puritan-Pilgrims. William Bradford was a leader of the Pilgrims, whose migration from England to New England serves as the point of origin for our Thanksgiving holiday. *Of Plymouth Plantation* tells the tale of the Pilgrims' harrowing journey from Old to New England, including the fears and struggles that dominated the colony's first years. Bradford gives firsthand account of the disease, widespread death, resource scarcity, uncertain relationships with the native Americans, and disruptive internal political contentions that taxed those Pilgrim settlers. When they got their colony on its feet, they celebrated their survival and the loving providence of God with a feast of thanksgiving, to which the natives were invited: "Our harvest being gotten in, . . . at which time, amongst other recreations, we exercised our arms, many of the Indians coming amongst us, . . . whom for three days we entertained and feasted."[1] Bradford's account was almost lost

---

1. Bradford, *Of Plymouth Plantation*, 100n8. While Bradford's journal makes an opaque nod to a "first thanksgiving," it is a letter by Edward Winslow that gives us this explicit description of the Pilgrims' celebration of the first successful harvest.

to us forever until someone rediscovered the manuscript in a British library, right before the Civil War. Since then, the story of the "first Thanksgiving" has become the template for American celebrations for generations.

Of Plymouth Plantation is a remarkably easy read for a text some 400 years old, and the tale it weaves is full of tension and intrigue, highs and lows. Jay Parini, an accomplished novelist, literary critic, and my colleague at Middlebury College, suggests in his book, *Promised Land: Thirteen Books that Changed America*, that *Of Plymouth Plantation* "might well be described as America's first immigration narrative," perhaps a fitting reminder of our immigrant origins in a national moment in which immigration is so widely politicized and stigmatized. Parini also suggests the book's power lies in its story, told in biblical proportions:

> Bradford begins *Of Plymouth Plantation* . . . with a tale of dispossession. His narrative is very much written like an Old Testament story, where God's people are driven off their land, suffer exile among heathens [that is, the Dutch], and go off in search of their own promised land in the New World. The whole mode of the unfolding story, its flavor and texture, will be familiar to anyone who has skimmed the five books of Moses.[2]

Of Plymouth Plantation remains a compelling read, because it weaves the quintessential tale of a people searching for God in their distress, as well as in their own striving.

Whenever I spend time with *Of Plymouth Plantation*, I am inevitably drawn again to a chapter in the story that occurs well before the all-too-brief summary of the mythical first Thanksgiving. Earlier in the book, Bradford includes a letter written to the Pilgrim party as they are preparing to leave England. The letter was written by John Robinson, a leader in the Puritan movement who was for some reason unable to travel with those Pilgrims to the New World. In his letter, Robinson dutifully gives his sisters and brothers advice on the kind of community they should strive to create. In a word, he urges them to establish a community that, in its character, exudes thanksgiving for the grace of God that will watch over them. Live gratefully as the redeemed people you know yourselves to be. Live gratefully. Robinson urges his Pilgrim friends to live their gratitude for all God's blessings.

Robinson goes on to suggest three specific ways in which this band of Pilgrims can form a grateful society: First, he warns them that "watchfulness must be had that we neither at all in ourselves do give, no, nor easily take offense being given by others."[3] Robinson warns his Pilgrim sisters

2. Parini, *Promised Land*, 12–13.
3. Bradford, *Of Plymouth Plantation*, 56.

and brothers that they will face disagreement and conflict. They will not always agree on who they should be or what they should do in this new society they will establish. In those times, he warns, you must exercise what he calls "brotherly forbearance" with one another. Here Robinson surely had in mind Paul's admonition in Romans 2, where the apostle suggests a failure to exercise grace with others is an affront to the grace God first extends to each and every one of us. Divisive judgmentalism is akin to despising the forbearance of God, for anyone who truly appreciates the grace God extends to us in our sin must extend that grace to others. A healthy society is one in which the fellowship of people navigate their different opinions and personalities with care and patience, never forgetting they are fellow pilgrims on the same journey. Without forbearance, every moment of disagreement or conflict will be an occasion for sowing mistrust between themselves and others, and Robinson warns them that no society can survive if fellow citizens treat one another as enemies. Rather than attacking every difference or assuming the worst in the other side, Robinson insists they take care not to give or take undue offense. Such forbearance marks a people as grateful to God.

Second, Robinson insists to his friends "that with your common employments you join common affections truly bent upon the general good."[4] You cannot go it alone on this harrowing journey, he reminds. A grateful society acknowledges that, and it responds to God's good gifts with equal dedication to the needs of others. In other words, a grateful society is one in which everyone seeks to pass their blessings onward, together working toward the common good. Sometimes that common good requires some sacrifice from our individual interests or pursuits. What we consider a right or an entitlement sometimes must yield to the obligation we have for the safety and good of others. But in the end, a society that prioritizes the common good is one in which everyone benefits, and we satisfy the mandate Jesus himself gives when he assures us that in feeding the hungry and welcoming the stranger and doing these things to the least among us, we extend grace to him. The common good, including the needs of those most vulnerable among us, is the focus of a grateful people.

Finally, Robinson cautions his friends that as they are setting up their community, "let your wisdom and godliness appear, not only in choosing such persons as do entirely love and will promote the common good, but also in yielding unto them all due honor and obedience in their lawful administrations."[5] If a civil community is to live into a commitment

4. Bradford, *Of Plymouth Plantation*, 57.
5. Bradford, *Of Plymouth Plantation*, 57.

to the common good, and thus to reflect gratitude to the Creator for all good gifts, then that community needs leaders who reflect those priorities. Choose leaders who are wise and godly, says Robinson. Choose leaders who understand themselves to be the beneficiaries of grace, who do not live under the delusion of being self-made but who comport themselves with gratitude and humility, and who lead people with wisdom and integrity toward the common good. Political leadership without moral integrity leads a people perfectly nowhere. John Robinson knew this, and so he implored his Pilgrim friends to choose from themselves leaders who would reflect the values they collectively cherished. And if they did that, they would be able to easily discharge their own responsibility to honor, obey, and respect the offices these leaders occupied.

I am struck by the timeliness of this very old advice. In our moment in American history, many Americans are despondent over the demise of any semblance of civility among our political leaders, increasingly too in our local communities, families, and churches. Hyper-partisan ideological opposition haunts nearly every engagement we undertake with kin, neighbors, and fellow citizens, making the risk of irreparable offense so weighty that the list of things we will not discuss in polite company becomes longer and longer. The tribalism that has overwhelmed our politics numbs our attention to the common good. Self-interest takes its place as the measure of what is right and good, and politicians exploit this moral coup by appealing to our baser instincts and pitting us against one another. Our political culture is perhaps more divisive than at any other time in American history (short of the Civil War), and the moral ethos has deteriorated to the point that the idea of visionary ethical leadership itself is suspect. Now even evangelical Christians, the defenders of "moral values" two decades ago, mortgage a commitment to ethical leadership in order to assure access to power. Given his morally questionable professional and personal behavior, President Trump would seem an odd fit for them, yet white evangelicals overwhelmingly voted for him because he promised long-desired victories on legislative and judicial priorities. Meanwhile, an impulse to divide and conquer has been the president's lifelong strategy, first in business and now in politics, making his election the fitting culmination of this divisive chapter in American history. These days we seem to be failing Robinson's vision for a virtuous society on all three fronts.

Perusing *Of Plymouth Plantation* during this national holiday reminds us of the higher moral aspirations that are foundational to the story of America. Robinson's admonitions are similar to those in a more famous Puritan sermon, "A Model of Christian Charity," preached by the Massachusetts Bay Colony governor John Winthrop sometime near the Puritans' arrival in the new world. From this sermon we get the phrase "a city upon a hill," made famous when Ronald Reagan co-opted it as a metaphor for American exceptionalism. (That more Americans associate this phrase with Reagan than with Winthrop is a sad testament to our detachment from our founding texts!) Preached by Winthrop generations before the United States anointed itself the global defender of democracy, Winthrop used the phrase to impress on his fellow Puritan immigrants the moral and religious importance of their experiment of community in Massachusetts.

Winthrop begins "A Model of Christian Charity" by acknowledging that human societies inevitably host differences in wealth and power. God invites us to govern ourselves with just social order, however, so that the differences between us might be mitigated in the name of the common good. To do so is an imperative of natural moral law and Christian conviction, a demand of justice and of mercy. Just order positions all of us to serve the common good and witness to the glory of God. In fact, if we shrink from our duty to glorify God through our practice of love, justice, mercy, and forbearance, Winthrop predicts God will abandon us to our own devices. This, in fact, is where he invokes that "city on a hill" metaphor, not to describe America as a beacon of democracy but to remind his Puritan community that the world watches to see if they will be faithful to their task:

> For we must consider that we shall be as a city upon a hill. The eyes of all people are upon us, so that if we shall deal falsely with our God in this work we have undertaken, and so cause him to withdraw his present help from us, we shall be made a story and a by-word through the world.[6]

Winthrop reminds his fellow Puritans that failure to live in a covenant of justice and mercy with one another will not only doom their community, it will proclaim to the world their faithlessness and make them (and their God) a global laughingstock. He urges them to take seriously their calling to live their allegiance to God in their fidelity to one another:

> Now the only way to avoid this shipwrack [sic], and to provide for our posterity, is to follow the counsel of Micah, to do justly, to love mercy, to walk humbly with our God. For this end, we must be knit together in this work as one man. We must entertain each other in brotherly affection, we must be willing to abridge ourselves of our superfluities, for the supply of others' necessities. We must uphold a familiar commerce together in all meekness, gentleness, patience, and liberality. We must delight in each other, make others' conditions our own, rejoice together,

6. Winthrop, "Model of Christian Charity," 91.

mourn together, labor and suffer together, always having before
our eyes our commission and community in the work, our community as members of the same body.[7]

This is the original recipe for that "city on a hill," a definition of American exceptionalism we appear to have lost.

To a band of Pilgrims committed to setting up a community in America, John Robinson and John Winthrop point out a timeless truth: you are
what you do. Actions and character reinforce one another. And if you want
to lay claim to being a godly society, a community grateful for the divine
grace that watches over it and protects it, then your actions will need to reflect that grace and godliness. Be right with God. Practice forbearance with
each other. Care for the common good. Choose and honor virtuous leaders.
Remember what binds you together—the grace of God—and practice the
virtues of thanksgiving, especially when things are not going well.

The Puritan ethic is an imperative that is inherently biblical: live with
one another (as the Letter to the Colossians puts it, "clothe yourselves") with
compassion, kindness, forbearance, and love, as an expression of thanksgiving for the grace God extends to us (Col 3:12). These days you will hear
plenty of public pulpiteers bellow a call for the United States to return to its
identity as a righteous nation, a Christian America. Many of the assumptions around a "Christian America" are problematic, including the simplistic
view of history on which the idea depends, its theological tone-deafness in
a religiously pluralistic nation, and the artificially specific and anachronistic
set of moral priorities (usually opposition to abortion and homosexuality)
its advocates claim as markers of our righteous heritage. To the degree, however, that we wish to claim Christian conviction as an important source of
American moral identity, Robinson and Winthrop give us clear indication
of what it means to be a righteous nation: live and care for one another with
the grace God first extends to us.

A day of thanksgiving is nice, but to be truly thankful requires more
than a single holiday and its momentary rhetoric. A truly thankful people
has gratitude in its bones; gratitude is the DNA of its being. Gratitude for
grace inspires our own exercise of grace with one another. Gratitude for
divine generosity inspires generosity toward the least in our midst. Gratitude for unconditional love inspires the embrace of the unwelcomed in our
proximity. Gratitude for God's reconciliation inspires the inclusion of the
alien and stranger within our boundaries. Gratitude to God, when authentic, becomes the character of a people and is reflected in the character of
their leaders.

7. Winthrop, "Model of Christian Charity," 91.

When we Americans celebrate Thanksgiving and hearken back to that first Pilgrim Thanksgiving long ago, we ought to do more than take a minute between the parade and the presentation of turkey to count our blessings. If we want to follow the template of our Pilgrim ancestors, our act of thanksgiving must take the form of a commitment to be a moral community—to live with one another in the grace that God first extended to us—and not just to our fellow citizens, but to the strangers in our midst and our neighbors around the world. Anyone who tempts us to redefine our social responsibilities as anything short of this kind of grace lived in the world, lived for the common good, stands in violation of both biblical principle and our national heritage.

I am well aware that our early history was more complicated than Bradford represents it. Neither the atrocities committed against native Americans nor those on African slaves is adequately represented in *Of Plymouth Plantation*, though they are inescapable parts of our larger national story. American history is morally complicated, and we must honor the truth of that dubious history and confront its consequences, consequences that remain part of who we are as a nation to this day. Yet I do not think the murkiness of our national history prevents us from revisiting earlier chapters of our story and extracting chastened lessons from it. The mythic tale of the first Thanksgiving reminds us of at least some of the better angels of our national origins. A vision of a society committed to the common good. Inclusive embrace of even the stranger. The deliberate practice of patience, forbearance, and mutual concern as collective character. Leaders who are chosen and respected for their virtue and wisdom. The regular habit of giving thanks for the good gifts we enjoy.

Thanksgiving is an act of moral community. Our Puritan heritage reminds us of that. What might it mean for Americans to give thanks this year as a genuine expression of gratitude, but also as a challenge to ourselves—to be a nation of virtue, of neighborliness, of forbearance, and of commitment to the common good, as those first Pilgrims imagined? At least for those of us who identify with biblical tradition, to take up that challenge is part of what it means to commit to the new life we are called to live in Christ, as an anthem of thanks to the God who first loved us, and as a witness to the world of God's grace and glory.

17

When Sarah Stops Laughing

(Christmas)

The Bible tells us Abraham and Sarah were old, *really* old, when God sent messengers to tell them that they were about to have a child. A laughable prospect at this time in their lives, thought Sarah. So impossible was it that she gave Abraham her maidservant so he might produce an heir with her. Abraham and Hagar did have a child, a son named Ishmael, but that surrogate birth only intensified Sarah's grief. Abraham now had a son but she did not, and Hagar never let her forget it. The contempt of her maidservant made her own barrenness nearly unendurable, but Sarah had long since accepted that there would be no good news, so when God's messengers suggested she would have a child, she could do nothing but laugh. She was embarrassed by her reaction, but it was her immediate response to such a preposterous suggestion. She laughed the skeptic's chortle, but soon it turned to the giggle of unbridled joy, for God kept the promise and she and Abraham had a son. They named him Isaac, appropriately enough, for the name means laughter. "God has brought laughter to me," sang Sarah, "everyone who hears will laugh with me" (Gen 21:6).

Many years later, in a story we encounter during Advent, the Bible tells us of a priest named Zechariah and his wife Elizabeth, also without children and getting up there in years. Though they had prayed for children and had been "righteous before God" in all their dealings, a family had never come, and they had long since given up hope. Their neighbors knew that Zechariah and Elizabeth were faithful to God, and so they felt bad for them. For her part, Elizabeth could not help but feel pressured by her community's expectations and disgraced by her inability to produce the child she and her husband wanted. Then one day an angel of the Lord appeared to Zechariah in the temple: "Do not be afraid," said the angel, "for your prayer has been heard. Your wife Elizabeth will bear you a son . . . You will have joy and gladness, and many will rejoice at his birth" (Luke 1:13–14). Understandably, Zechariah voiced skepticism over this announcement, and that was not the response the angel wanted to hear, so Zechariah was struck mute until the day the Lord's promise was fulfilled. That promise came to pass and Elizabeth bore a son, whom they named John. She and Zechariah gave praise to God, and all their neighbors rejoiced with them.

Abraham and Sarah, Rebekah and Isaac, Jacob and Rachel, the parents of Samson, Hannah (mother of the prophet Samuel), Elizabeth and Zechariah—all prayed for an end to their "barrenness" (as it was referred to then), and God delivered, literally. Theirs are well-known biblical stories of miracles and answered prayers. For some of us, though, these stories ring hollow. In the United States alone, one out of every ten couples struggles with infertility, and many people in nontraditional relationships experience multiple physical, legal, and logistical impediments to the desire to have a baby. While time and technology sometimes yield positive results, often the story of infertility does not end happily. From a faith perspective, infertility raises many questions, especially given the way it is depicted in our sacred texts. What are we to do when the promise is unfulfilled in our lives? What is the right response when the Bible suggests a pattern that our circumstances refuse to follow? What is next when Hannah's prayers are not answered, Zechariah's petitions are ignored, and Sarah stops laughing?

My spouse Elizabeth (the righteous irony of her name lost on neither of us) and I asked these kinds of questions for years. As we mourned our own infertility, part of the ordeal was the struggle to make sense of the hopelessness, powerlessness, and absence of any good news, especially in the context of biblical faith. We looked in vain for a sacred story to identify with, but there seemed to be no scriptural template for what we endured. Every case of infertility in the Bible concludes with a happy ending: faithful servants get pregnant, everyone rejoices in the miracle, and God receives unending praise. In the world we were inhabiting, the story did not progress quite that way. Piety and prayer went unrewarded, month after month, then year after year. With all due respect to Sarah, infertility was no laughing matter for us.

One part of the biblical stories was accurate enough to us, however. Infertility brings incredible emotional pain. All of the women and many of the men in these stories openly mourned the absence of children. Sarah's sorrow over her infertility was aggravated by Hagar's success; just the presence of her maidservant's son Ishmael served as an excruciating reminder of what Sarah herself could not have. Similarly, Elizabeth and I found our own sadness intensified by reminders everywhere of unsatisfied longing. While we prayed year after year for a child, we watched siblings easily start their own families. We constantly battled the envy that is stoked by witnessing everyone around you having children, sometimes children who were not planned. While our friends and family members were having kids at will, or even by dumb luck, we could not buy a pregnancy. Friendships were strained as couples we were accustomed to seeing socially found themselves suddenly preoccupied with an experience to which we could not relate. Family gatherings became an endurance test, compulsory immersions in the reminders of our failures.

Christmas was the hardest, for this holiday is arguably the most depressing time of the year to be dealing with infertility. With each passing Christmas spent not pregnant, the sense of loss cut deeper and deeper, so that finally one year we just could not bear to buy presents for our young nephews. Just entering a Toys-R-Us made us uncontrollably depressed. The theologian Miroslav Volf describes his and his wife's experience with infertility at Christmastime in a way that certainly resonates with me:

> "For unto us a child is born, unto us a son is given," I would hear read or sung in hundreds of different variations. But from me a child was withheld. The miracle of Mary's conception, the rejoicing of the heavens at her newborn child, the exultation of Elizabeth all became signs of God's painful absence, not God's advent . . . If God's Son indeed was in charge, it seemed that he didn't care to move even his royal finger in our favor. At Christmas, I felt like the only child in a large family to whom the parents had forgotten to give gifts.[1]

The Christmas season is when the church's ritualization of pregnant expectation conspires with culture's nostalgia for wondrous childhoods to provide a potent reminder of the hole in your life. The Christmas proclamation, "to you is born this day," felt a bit like a tease as we were waiting in vain for our own.

Christmas is a nightmare while you are immersed in the unrequited desire for a child, but a close second on the pain scale is going to church on

1. Volf, "Gift of Infertility," 33.

Mother's Day. In the South, where we lived for a decade, Mother's Day is a holy day on par with none other. One church we attended liturgically commemorated the day by presenting flowers to every woman in attendance, all the "moms and potential moms," an exercise dripping with sexism but also excruciating for those facing the reality that they did not possess the potential assumed to be universal. That cultural celebration of reproductive success and flourishing families, Mother's Day became for us a Sunday to skip church and go for a ride alone.

While we chafed against the happily-ever-after theme of those biblical stories of long-awaited pregnancies, we did recognize the emotional pain they conveyed, as well as the social pressure that exacerbates the pain of infertility. Just as the need for male heirs created intense pressure on the heroes and heroines in Scripture, so today our culture demands that adults having children be the norm, and scientific advances intensify the push to do whatever it takes to get that family. Moralists who study the ethics of reproductive technologies call this the "reproductive imperative," the cultural pressure (especially on women) to have children. The reproductive imperative drives our society's fascination with technological advancements in assisted reproduction, procedures like *in vitro* fertilization. Despite the optimistic press given to these technologies, they are successful in about one out of every four cases at best, and their cost (and the general unwillingness of insurance companies to cover them) makes them prohibitive to many, and a financial stress on those who can afford them. Yet assisted reproduction remains a spry industry, egged on (excuse the pun) by the social message that in order to be complete and fulfilled human beings, we all need children who carry our genes.

Yes, despite their implicit and annoying optimism, one thing the biblical stories get right is the pain and pressure that descend upon those who struggle with infertility. Sarah was constantly irritated by her rivalry with a more fertile Hagar, and the story suggests Hagar knew how to rub it in. Similarly, Hannah agonized over her infertility to the point that she could neither eat nor sleep, and the provocations of her husband's other, more fertile, wife did not help. Thankfully, neither Elizabeth nor I endured a lack of consideration from rival concubines, but less intentionally the words of friends and family members produced similar irritation. Strangers ask you whether you have a family *yet*, with helpful emphasis on your tardiness. Friends and family members push you on when you are finally going to get on with the baby thing, pastors interrogate your family plans, and everyone acts as if getting pregnant is a simple matter of volition—you have a baby when you *want* to.

It may be worse when people know about your struggles with infertility, though. The number of people with children who told me they understood what we were going through was mind-blowing. Some people say it because they do not know what else to say, and they are desperate to sound sympathetic. Some people say it because they know someone else who went through it, as if a kind of mathematical transitive property gives one access to the pain infertility causes. Some people claim to know what you are going through because they too had "a little trouble" conceiving, assuming that a temporary requirement of patience approximates dealing with the reality of knowing you'll *never* get pregnant. Excuse me, but even if it took you forever and a day, if your story ends with giving birth you cannot know what it is like to look into the future and see no reason to hope. The fact that you did not get pregnant on your precise timetable is not equivalent to being forced to come to terms with the fact that your dream of giving birth to a child is never going to be fulfilled.

Which brings us back to our problem. Like that friend who thinks she can relate while she changes her baby's socks, the Bible seems to respond to our plight with nothing but tales with happy endings. What good is biblical faith when it seems clear that Zechariah's prayer will not be answered this time? Where am I supposed to find spiritual solace in a text that implies that everyone who prays will get what they want? What do we do when the Bible's stories do not match our own experiences, when life invokes a sob instead of a laugh?

From the perspective of Christian faith, we could respond a number of ways, and a couple of these responses are, put bluntly, terrible things to say to another person. Yet I heard each of these terrible options in conversations with family and friends wrought with good intentions. Some kind hearts suggested that the solution is to stay positive. "Oh, it will happen," they confidently asserted. "You just need to have faith." I have never had much patience for a piety of positive thinking, and infertility only confirmed to me that this kind of theological naivety is shallow and dangerous. Evidence abounds that the faithful do not always get what they need or prayerfully request, the saccharine preaching of prosperity gospelers be damned. Other folks suggested it just was not God's will that we get pregnant. What in the world am I to do with that information? Besides peddling a picture of God as micromanager that I increasingly find dubious, bludgeoning someone with providence does nothing but reinforce the message that even God is against us when we suffer.

That insinuation is exactly contrary to the message of the gospel, of course, as we are reminded every Christmas season. The message of Christmas is the good news of Emmanuel, God-with-us, the assurance that God is with us intimately and lovingly, in the depths of our despair as much as in the heights of our prosperities. That good news of Emmanuel is the only takeaway I learned to read in these otherwise counterproductive biblical stories of infertility. Yes, Sarah, Rebekah, Hannah, and Elizabeth all got pregnant, but perhaps that is not the fundamental point. Perhaps the more basic assertion of these stories is that God is actively present in our suffering and sadness. Sometimes life hands us what we want, and sometimes not, but all the time God is there. In fact, Jesus' choice of company throughout his life suggests God is *more* present where there is suffering. The ill, injured, lonely, and ostracized were the kinds of people Emmanuel was especially keen on befriending, assuring them of God's love. A gospel of God-with-us does not guarantee the deepest yearnings of our hearts will be ours if we just pray harder. It does assure us, however, that God will walk with us in triumph and disappointment, and that neither good fortune nor bad can separate us from God.

As the apostle Paul put it in Romans 8, in a passage strangely bursting with birth and adoption imagery, "the sufferings of this present time are not worth comparing with the glory about to be revealed to us." Paul assures us that as we suffer through our present darkness, we can do so with hope, because the Spirit of God knows the deepest recesses of our hearts, "intercedes with sighs too deep for words," and shows us glimpses of a future that still includes God's enduring presence. While Paul confidently asserts "all things work together for good for those who love God," he does not promise that the good to which all things conspire is the very thing for which we pray. Instead the good to which all things work together on our behalf is that steadfastness of God, the assurance that God is for us and therefore no one or nothing shall ultimately stand against us. The good that gets us through trials and tragedies is not our specific wish, but the promise that neither "hardship, or distress, or persecution, or famine, or nakedness, or peril, or sword" will neutralize God's power to be present and to comfort us as we need. "Neither death, nor life, nor angels, nor rulers, nor things present, nor things to come, nor powers, nor height, nor depth, nor anything else in all creation, will be able to separate us from the love of God in Christ Jesus our Lord." *Nothing* will separate us from the love of God in Christ our Lord—not even the scarring disappointment of infertility.

In fact, sometimes the doors that close so painfully before us leads to the opening of other passageways into that Emmanuel love. I have a good friend who adores kids and occasionally nods toward her disappointment of having never had a family of her own. But she channels that pent-up love toward the children in her extended family, and her singleness has made her an especially good minister to older adults in a way that has enriched her vocationally and personally and has blessed the people who call her pastor (as well as those of us who call her friend). Even through her disappointment over doors unopened, she reflects the presence of God in her life.

For Elizabeth and me, the door that closed on pregnancy opened us to the wonderful and challenging world of adoption. Adoption has impressed upon us how true it is that children are gifts, precisely because they did not come to us easily or biologically. Adoption expanded our horizons to include an intercultural connectedness and an appreciation for neurodiversity that we did not possess before. In adoption we have learned a deeper respect for how inextricably tied are fortune and tragedy, as the faces of our children persistently remind us that our blessing came at the cost of others' pain and loss. In the joy and challenges that resulted from our infertility, we have discovered Paul's maxim to be true, that nothing can separate us from the love of God. Our proof is two young men from South Korea parked on our couch right now, playing Xbox together. They are the faces of Emmanuel to us.

As we Presbyterians attest in one of our church confessions, "In life and in death, we belong to God."[2] In personal challenges like the struggle with infertility, comfort comes in the knowledge that whatever life throws our way, God has us by the belt loops. God has us through the sadness, the anger, even the temptation to tell God to shove it. Through all of it, God holds us in providential care, and when we are ready, God is there to open us to holy resources of comfort, to new and amazing blessings we did not know to covet, and to surprises made possible by the doors that close on us. The good news in those biblical stories of triumph over barrenness, and in our story graced a different way, is God's awesome ability to transform (in Volf's words) the "poison" of infertility into "a gift, God's strange gift."[3] In the human faces of that strange gift, we see God-with-us, Emmanuel, working all along.

---

2. "Brief Statement of Faith," 11.1.
3. Volf, "Gift of Infertility," 33.

18

Along for the Ride

(Christmas)

Joseph should be considered the patron saint of parents raising children by adoption. An angel of the Lord came to Joseph and explained to him that he was about to be a father, but the child would not be his biological heir. It would not be an open adoption, so he could not tell anyone about the peculiar circumstances around his family formation. Finally, he needed to know that this kid would be a bit different. He will not respond to the world around him in the way kids conventionally do, warned the angel. He will relate to you differently. He is going to have an impulsive streak; do not be surprised if he just wanders away from you in the temple someday and misses the caravan home. Oh, and as he grows up, he is going to have a bit of a savior-complex—because he is one. Throw out the manual on this one, Joseph. By all accounts, Joseph got handed responsibility for raising a child who fell somewhat outside what is covered in the *Idiot's Guide to Parenting*.

In some ways, I can relate to Joseph. I am father to two wonderful sons, both of whom Elizabeth and I adopted from South Korea. Adoption has been a delightful experience for us as parents. It has made us more deliberate about—and grateful for—our roles as parents than we suspect we would have been had our children come to us as biological entitlement. Adoption has invited us to be intentionally multicultural, and we actively work to incorporate Korean food, holidays, and culture into our predominantly Pennsylvania Dutch traditions. Adoption also has made us better citizens and social critics by sharpening our radar for the ways that American society (and the church, for that matter) discriminates against people of color as well as individuals with physical, mental, and emotional differences.

Building a family through adoption has its challenges, though. There are things we do not know about the first days or months of our children's lives. They each have connections that extend well beyond us, to people and a culture who birthed them, which they need help understanding amidst the moral ambiguity that surrounds adoption. The joy they bring us comes by way of tragedy, for they bless our lives only because they have been separated from a family halfway around the world, and we know that the injuries that result from such separation can have real physiological, mental, and emotional impact on them as persons. In addition, each of my sons came to us with issues that fall within that broad category known as "special needs," some of them physical and some neurobiological, and those add another layer of daily challenge to raising our kids and directing them to a future of flourishing. Aggravating that layer of complexity in our family are the liabilities of the American health care system, especially in a resource-scarce environment like Vermont, where what our children need is too often unavailable or inadequately covered by insurance.

These needs present almost daily challenges to them as individuals and to our whole family, but of course there is much more to my boys than the obstacles that accompany them through life. First and foremost, they are great kids. Our older son is a creative (if reluctant) writer, an exciting athlete, and an informational sponge. His ability to absorb and regurgitate sports data should make him a coveted asset for ESPN someday, or perhaps the engine behind some athletic program's recruiting staff. His social courage renders him a nice complement to his clinically introverted parents, while also making him one hell of a salesman, as our church has discovered during several of its fundraisers. Our younger son has an acute emotional radar, a side-splitting sense of humor, and an admirably empathetic character. He also managed to earn his black belt in Tae Kwan Do by the age of ten, despite limb differences that others might see as a natural impediment.

My boys are awesome kids, but I often find myself challenged in my responsibility to care for them. Some of that challenge derives specifically from the lived experience of adoption, and some of it comes more broadly from the awesome responsibility parents universally have for the other human beings in their care. Some of the ways in which parenting challenges me, however, stem from my own limits and shortcomings. My sons often need precisely what I struggle most as a human being to offer. I am hopelessly impatient with other people and obsessively task-oriented, character traits that do not serve me well when the order of the day is waiting by a bedside or living with the uncertainty of long-term medical issues. I crave order and quiet time, rarities in any home with teenage boys, but especially absent when one of them cannot even compute the need for personal space. Too often I lack sufficient empathy, as well as the necessary brain filter that prompts a normal person to ask whether they should really say what they are thinking. That lack of filter results in what euphemistically might be called tough love, but in truth is more likely unconstructive "negative reinforcement." These deficiencies in character are exacerbated by the knowledge gulf required to navigate the complexities of both adoption and special needs. Elizabeth and I operate daily on the frontiers of competence in medicine and psychology, meaning that most days we feel like we simply do not know what we are doing. I love my boys to death, but I often feel like I am in over my head in raising them, ill-equipped in knowledge and in character to help them grow into the adults they will be.

I imagine Joseph knew exactly what I feel as a parent. The kid he discovered to be suddenly in his charge could not have been easy for him to raise. Joseph had to swallow hard just to receive the news that he was a father. Absent almost any details about him, we often imagine Joseph as a dutiful man, responsibly taking charge of Mary and this child and caring for the well-being of both. But as Scripture tells the story, not all of his choices were noble. When he found out that she was going to have a baby, Joseph refused to subject Mary to public disgrace, but he apparently considered putting her out quietly, which still would have been the end to this young woman in a culture that did not embrace extramarital pregnancy. After he accepted his responsibility, his first major decision seems to have been to drag Mary, nine months pregnant, on a donkey to Bethlehem. When strange wise men from faraway lands visited the new Messiah and his mother, Joseph apparently was away from home. And when he took the family on a trip to the temple, he managed to leave the city without his son. For all we know, Joseph struggled his whole life to fulfill the awesome responsibility of parenting his beloved adopted child.

Maybe he felt consistently in over his head, raising a boy who bucked all conventions, a kid whose history and identity were inaccessible to him, a child who did not respond in any of the "normal" ways children respond. We know almost nothing about the man, so maybe he too felt that he was constitutionally ill-suited for the extraordinary duties presented by this adoption. Maybe he concluded he was no match for this responsibility, and perhaps he even resented being put in this position. I can imagine him bristling when people unhelpfully minimized his son's differences by reminding him that "all children are challenges." I can relate to Joseph's likely irritation when friends with good intentions delegitimized the genuine struggles in his family by assuring him they went through the exact same things, even though he knew for a fact they did not. I can feel him chafing when people passive-aggressively pointed out the weird or disruptive things his Jesus was doing and implied Junior's nonconformity was a product of bad parenting. Surely Joseph grew frustrated with the rarity of signs that his parenting was doing any good at all. He had to have felt insufficiently equipped for the challenges that came with being an adoptive parent in these circumstances.

And yet he did it. He fulfilled the duties of fatherhood and raised Jesus to be the person he was supposed to be, with love and care. He may not have been a super-dad or a super-husband; we cannot know for sure, because the Bible gives him little press. His relatively small role in the gospel story contributes to the impression Joseph himself may have harbored, that he was just along for the ride in this crazy story, clearly the inferior parent, as often a liability to family dynamics as a genuine help to his loving spouse. Nonetheless, he stepped up to the challenge, because the angel promised him that in this child he would see the face of God. "She will bear a son, and you are to name him Jesus, for he will save his people from their sins" (Matt 1:21). Despite the uncertainty, frustration, and worry, every time Joseph looked at his child, he saw his own salvation. Many of us who are parents look into the eyes of our children and see the same thing, glimpses of the saving grace of God.

I cannot help but think that those of us who adopt see that grace in deeper colors than biological parents, precisely because of the pain, sadness, complication, and murkiness through which the beauty of our children emerges. There is something sacramental about the experience of parenting, but especially parenting children through adoption. Building on St. Augustine's definition of a sacrament as "the visible sign of God's invisible grace," John Calvin described sacramental experience as the "outward sign by which the Lord seals on our consciences the promises of [God's] good will toward us."[1] Our Protestant forefathers insisted there were only two Sacraments that warrant the capital S, for only Baptism and Eucharist were practices that could be traced back to the earliest church. Calvin, however, gave us permission to think about sacramental experience more broadly, with a little s, beyond the practices specific to church to include other experiences of visible nature that confirm to us the reality of God's invisible grace. "The term 'sacrament,'" he wrote, "embraces generally all those signs which God has ever enjoined upon men [sic] to render them more certain and confident of

1. Calvin, Institutes, 1277.

the truth of his promises."[2] Sometimes these sacramental experiences come in the form of apparent miracles, but other times they are signs of an invisible grace we encounter in "natural things." Calvin's favorite example was the rainbow that appeared to Noah, but I think his definition of sacramental experience is an apt representation of parenting too.

A sacrament is a physical metaphor that signals God's presence to us, and that does so precisely because the visible sign is so external, so other than the mystical grace for which it stands. Something as mundane as bread, wine, or water requires intentional reflection to become for us the body, blood, or blessing of God. Because the elements are so external, to experience them sacramentally requires us to do something, to complete an act, to discover and feel the mystical connections between sign and signified, and to dwell in the profundity of the elements' dual character. In its very externality, sacrament draws us into intentional reflection on the promise of God's goodwill toward us and seals it on our soul.

In similar fashion, adoption offers a sacramental encounter with God's loving inclination toward us at a depth biological child-rearing cannot access, precisely because of the "both-and" nature of the relationship, biological strangers who are also our familial intimates. I certainly do not mean to suggest that there is nothing holy in biological parenting, but in the experience of adoption we exist in another metaphorical plane. The very externality of the relationship we forge with children who simultaneously are ours but not ours requires us to intentionally seek and experience the divine grace we encounter in those relationships. Adoption as sacrament prompts a special occasion for thanksgiving, but it also demands an extraordinary level of commitment. In this way, adoption resembles that other function Calvin identified in the sacraments, their service as a means by which we "attest our piety toward God."[3] Adoption provides us especially poignant reminders of God-with-us, just as it offers constant opportunity to affirm our gratitude to the Giver by giving ourselves to vulnerable others, strangely now in our care.

Experiencing our children sacramentally, we are reminded that they are conduits for receiving and expressing God's love, even in the harder hours of parenting. The endurance we and our children must develop, the frustrations we inevitably feel along the way, the palpable awareness of our own mistakes and shortcomings, especially in the face of the needs our children bring to our task—in all these ways, when we regard our children sacramentally, they are occasions to celebrate the realities of forgiveness and

2. Calvin, *Institutes*, 1294.

3. Calvin, *Institutes*, 1277.

grace and the new days God extends, empowering us to live imperfectly the calling to care for the children given unto us.

Calvin reassures us that God gives us the gift of sacraments precisely because God knows we stumble and need constant reminder of the divine promise to catch us. "Our faith is slight and feeble," says Calvin; "unless it be propped on all sides and sustained by every means, it trembles, wavers, totters, and at last gives way."[4] The uncertainty of step Calvin describes here is an accurate description of the daily experience of adoptive parenting, yet he assures us God gives us visible signs of God's "infinite kindness" for precisely this need. If we are open to seeing them with the eyes of faith, God reinforces the promises of grace in tangible ways, to prop us up in our moments of "ignorance and dullness" and "weakness." If we are open to seeing it with the eyes of faith, the promise of grace shines forth in our children, giving us the hope to persist precisely through those moments when we are least sure we are doing them any good at all.

This seems to me a particularly good message to hear at Christmas. The Christmas gospel is that into a world wrought with violence, chaos, and sadness came a child who embodied God's promise to be present with us and steadfast in love. That child was Emmanuel, the assurance of God-with-us, a gift made to his adoptive father on all our behalf. In the spirit of Emmanuel, perhaps we are called to see smaller glimpses of God-with-us as Joseph did, in our own children. To understand them this way is to infuse sacramental meaning into the whole of the Christmas season, even the aspects of holiday we bemoan as excessively commercialized and commodified. Children at Christmas convey joy in gift-giving and gift-receiving, trust in the mysteries they await on Christmas night and the reliable goodness of ol' St. Nick, love in the fleeting reclamation of family time, and peace in the possibility that, for one night at least, nothing matters more than the anticipation of presents under the tree. Joy, faith, love, and peace—in the authenticity children bring to the whole experience of Christmas, they show us truth and goodness. They are to us the visible signs of God's invisible grace.

Joseph was more than along for the ride. Shrouded from us by history, he nonetheless played an essential role in God's redemptive story. Christmas is that holy season when we celebrate Emmanuel, God-with-us, God coming into our world. It is only appropriate, then, that this season also be so fundamentally about children, for they are daily reminders of Emmanuel in our lives. In the good and the challenges of being parent, grandparent, guardian, or church family, we discover children are the visible signs of invisible grace, especially in those moments when we are most in need of

---

4. Calvin, *Institutes*, 1278.

grace. Children are our hope for God's future. Their future is the good fight to which we have been called, the race in which we persevere. Their faces are the signs of our salvation, our investment in God's reign. We, too, are instruments of grace when we undertake the mundane, messy, frustrating tasks of caring for children. Grace does not come to us easily, without complication, challenges, or risk. But it comes, consistently and wonderfully. To receive it in the face of a child for whom we are responsible is to embrace an angelic charge, the calling to participate in our own redemption.

ORDINARY TIME

19

God in the Hurricane

I love the book of Job, for Job is the place in the Bible for cranks like me. You may know the story, but a quick review nonetheless: the book of Job imagines a wager between God and Satan, where Satan bets God that if the comfortable and pious Job were deprived of his fortunes long enough, his fidelity to God would crumble and he would curse God. God puts his money on Job and the wager is on, as God allows Satan to inflict Job's family, financial circumstances, and physical health with trial after trial. Job suffers mightily, and when he responds, he is not the "patient Job" we are taught to expect in the story. He takes his suffering without abandoning God, but he does not do so quietly. He complains, going on at length about the undeserved circumstances he is enduring. The perceived injustice of Job's plight makes him cranky, and God is cranky right back at him, responding to Job's laments and accusations with a perfectly toned "you don't know what you're talking about, little man." God thunders from the whirlwind, "Who is this that darkens counsel by words without knowledge? Gird up your loins like a man, I will question you, and you shall declare to me" (Job 38:2–3). With the power of a natural disaster, God reminds Job of his limited perspective and the profundity of mysteries in both heaven and earth. Job is forced to admit the arrogance of his presumption that he deserved better than the lot he had been cast. He admits that in his complaint he had spoken of "things too wonderful" for himself (Job 42:3). Ultimately God reminds Job that God is God and he is not, and that it is beyond the capacity of the human to perfectly understand the complexities of life that visit us.

The book of Job tries to take seriously something with which we all struggle, the reality that bad things happen to good people, and it can be hard to locate meaning in the unfortunate things that life inflicts upon us. The question of why bad things happen to good people is as old as the human community, of course. The senselessness of tragedy often produces culture-wide angst when the injury is significant enough. When hurricanes devastate whole sections of the country, or when school shootings put us all on edge, Americans of many religious persuasions or none at all find themselves looking for the purpose that makes our loss something more than pointless. What I love about the book of Job is it refuses to answer our need for explanation easily; in fact, you could argue it refuses to offer explanation at all. Job asks God for a justification of his misfortune, and what he gets in return is a lesson on the grandness of the cosmos and the smallness of human perspective. In the terrifying reminder of this disparity, Job cannot help but confess he is guilty of considering things too wonderful for himself.

We Christians experience tragedy our own way, of course, with the requirement that it jibe somehow with our profession of faith in an all-powerful and ever-loving God. Why does this God allow bad things to happen to good people? How is the suffering of the righteous fair or good? If you watch the news regularly, it is hard to resist Job's question. One act of gun violence after another rocks American communities, so much so that the number of Americans killed by mass violence in some years rivals the number of American casualties in the armed forces. Natural disasters and global pandemics threaten millions of innocent people. Terrorism inflicted on families at our southern border separates parents from children, traumatizes refugees who already are victims of poverty and violence, and dehumanizes people because of the happenstance of their birthplace. Vicious political, cultural, and racial divisions continue in this country. On top of what we see in the news, many of us carry medical concerns, personal crises, and the loss of dear friends, and the weight of all this suffering is aggravated by the apparent disconnect between a world of chaos and the weekly affirmations we share in church that God is all goodness and love. Where, then, is God in all of the pain?

Among Christians there are a few standard answers, two of which I find especially unsatisfying. Many of us have heard it said in trying times that suffering and the things that cause it happen according to God's will. It is God's will that my dear friend died when he did. It is God's will that you are going through financial hardship. From time to time, we also hear God's will invoked in response to tragic events in the nation or world. For example, immediately after 9/11, a number of allegedly Christian televangelists claimed the terrorist attack was God's will, divine punishment on a nation that had abandoned God in its embrace of homosexuality and its permissive attitude toward abortion. Some of these same rascals claimed divine clairvoyance again after Hurricane Katrina laid waste to New Orleans in 2005.

I find this invocation of God's will as a response to tragedy misguided in the best of cases, repulsive in some formulations. Those who play the "God's will" card sometimes use it as an opportunity to attribute their own narrow judgmentalism to God, as in the case when certain Christian leaders explained Hurricane Harvey as God's retribution on Houston for its tolerance of LGBTQ people. The meanness in this explanation says more about its barely human spokesmen than it does about the God disclosed to us in Jesus Christ.

Others who invoke God's will on occasions like these do so for more purely theological reasons, as a defense of God's sovereignty. For them the logic of belief in an all-powerful God requires that we tag God with responsibility for the bad stuff that happens as well as the good. We may not know why God does what God does, but belief in an all-powerful God requires that we admit God does it all, the good and the bad. Pastorally speaking, though, it is not at all helpful to tell people in their moment of struggle that somehow God wants them to suffer. Is that "assurance" really supposed to make us feel better? Does it serve as balm in our tragedy to imagine God as the one pulling the trigger, spreading the disease, or summoning the hurricane? Are we so certain the tragedy we endure is what God wants for us? God does not often leave a note, so the presumption to speak for God in those circumstances is just that—presumption, and particularly harmful presumption at that.

The great preacher William Sloane Coffin, in what was probably the hardest sermon he had to deliver, addressed this very complaint when he rose to the pulpit soon after his own son died in a tragic automobile accident. In his week of mourning, Coffin had endured one too many well-intentioned visitors who were intent on reassuring him his loss was the will of God:

> For some reason, nothing so infuriates me as the incapacity of seemingly intelligent people to get it through their heads that God doesn't go around this world with fingers on triggers, his fist around knives, his hands on steering wheels . . . My own

consolation lies in knowing that it was *not* the will of God that
Alex die; that when the waves closed over the sinking car, God's
heart was the first of all our hearts to break.[1]

God's response to Job is also a rebuke to those today who would explain tragedy with callous reference of God's will. To do so is lazy and arrogant theology.

I am not sure the language of God's intention is even the right language
to use in moments like these. The idea that God has ulterior motives and is
working them out in our personal trials strikes me as an unjustified exag-
geration of the personal language we use for God. We Christians talk of
God as a person in large part because it is what we are. We have a natural
human need to translate God's unknowable nature into something we can
imagine. For this reason, the need to describe God with personal attributes
is understandable, and it is theologically justifiable insofar as God's own
"translation" of the divine came in the form of the human, namely Jesus
Christ. Permission to talk of God in human terms lies at the heart of the
Christian belief system, in the doctrine of the incarnation. But there are limits to what human analogies can capture of the reality of God. There is a hiddenness to God too, aspects of God that extend well beyond the metaphors
we muster to filter the experience of God for our own comprehension. God
is bigger than we are, and from time to time the language we use for God
implies more than we have reason to confidently claim about God and our
knowledge of God. Sometimes personal language for God risks exaggerat-
ing the similarities between us and God, and I suspect this preoccupation
with "God's will" or "God's intent" behind all of the tragedies we experience
is one of those times when the language of our faith tempts us to say things
too wonderful for ourselves.

If I generally break out in hives when someone starts talking assuredly
about God's will in the bad things that happen to good people, I also react
viscerally to the opposite claim. Sometimes, as a counter to those folks who
have such a confident read on God's will, other Christians will claim just
as surely that God has nothing to do with the tragedies that befall us. God
has nothing to do with natural disasters killing innocent people, they claim.
God has nothing to do with a friend getting cancer, or a nation inflicted
with trauma. But I do not see why these well-meaning declarations should
be uttered any more confidently. How do we know that God's will has *nothing* to do with the bad things that happen? Christians who insist on God's
distance from our tragedies usually do so in an attempt to absolve God of
any wrongdoing. If those prone to assign every jot and tittle to God's will do

---

1. Coffin, "Alex's Death," 263–64; italics original.

so as a defense of God's sovereign power, then those who insist God is not the cause of our tragedies do so as shield around God's reputation for love. A God of love surely would not intend for us to be as miserable as the dark days of human experience make us.

If God is the animating force behind all of life, however, it does not make theological sense to imply God was on vacation when tragedy hits, conveniently absolved of all responsibility. I also do not find it particularly helpful, pastorally speaking, to imply God is absent in our hardest moments, or somehow just not up to the task of delivering us from them. To claim categorically that my suffering is not God's intention suggests God is as much an innocent, helpless bystander as I am in those circumstances, and that is not exactly reassuring. It also is presumptuous, because from our limited human perspective we cannot know for certain that God has *no* hand in our tragedy, any more than we can say for sure that God directed it all to happen in detail. Both the flat assignment of tragedy to God and the insistence that God is innocent of it are forms of Job's folly, conveying insufficient respect for the mysteries of the cosmos and the hiddenness of God. They are examples of saying things too wonderful for ourselves.

But if I cannot pinpoint God's intentions either way, what can I say about God and the tragedies I witness, observe, or endure? I think I can say this: the world is bigger and more complex than we will ever understand; mysteries that elude human comprehension are real; and circumstances that inflict us with a sense of powerlessness and helplessness remind us of the scale of the cosmos and our place in it. Natural disasters check our arrogant assumption of scientific control over nature and our consumerist entitlement to the natural world, reminding us that we live largely at the earth's mercy. Disease points out to us just how much of living and dying we do not control. There is much in the world and about life that is too wonderful for us to speak of intelligently. Believe it or not, I find that check on perspective to be a helpful reminder, even if it is profoundly uncomfortable when it impresses itself on my reality.

Perhaps more comforting, even if I do not know the precise causal relationship God has with all of the bad stuff I see or experience, even if I cannot know for sure the extent to which the bad things that happen to and around me align with "God's will," I do know when tragedy occurs, God is there. I know God is there in the quiet of a hospital room. God is there in the terror of a natural disaster. God is there in the trauma of oppression and injustice, and God is there on the front lines of its opposition. My confidence that God is there with me and others in our suffering is borne out by the assurances of St. Paul, who insisted that "neither death, nor life, nor angels, nor rulers, nor things present, nor things to come, nor powers, nor height, nor depth, nor anything else in all creation, will be able to separate us from the love of God in Christ Jesus our Lord" (Rom 8:38–39). My confidence that God is present at ground zero in our traumas and tragedies lies in the promises of faith, in the message of incarnation and the symbol of the cross. Meeting us in the person of Christ, God made covenant with the human community to be God-with-us. Going to the cross, God reassures us there is no degree of suffering in which we will suddenly find God absent, no hard moment when we will lack for divine embrace. My confidence that God meets us in our hard moments is rooted in the story of Jesus, who embodied the good news that God is with us, especially on roads that lead to suffering and death.

I also am confident that God in Christ can be found standing with us in our tragedies because when I look, I often find the *body* of Christ there. This is what it means for the church to be church, that we are called to be ambassadors of God's presence with other human beings in their tragedies. God walks with people in their personal trials when we do. God stands with the marginalized through acts of injustice when we do. God stands with human beings enduring natural or manmade disaster when other people of goodwill rise up to help and heal. To be the church is to volunteer, explicitly and knowingly, to serve as conduits for God's presence in the world. *People* are a way for God to be with us in the tragedies of life, and the church is the community that deliberately commits to being this divine presence, the body of Christ, for others in the world.

I do not know why God lets bad things happen to good people. I actually doubt that is even the right question to ask. What I do know is this: the world is big and mysterious, life is complicated and hard, and sometimes "stuff" happens. But through it all, I truly believe God is with us. God abides with us, in good times and in bad. God embraces us, in the serenity of the sun and in the havoc of the hurricane. My confidence in God's enduring presence stems in part from how often I see God in the presence of God's people (Christian and otherwise), ministering to folks in the lowest moments of their existence. God is there when we are there for each other. I think that is enough for me. Everything else risks speaking things too wonderful for myself.

20

Holy War on Hate

In the spring of 2019, fifty-one people were killed in an act of terror on two mosques in Christchurch, New Zealand. The victims' only crime was gathering as Muslims for prayer. The attack was perpetrated by a man who identified as a white nationalist, part of the resistance to an alleged global effort to exterminate white people. His manifesto, meant to inspire others in the cause, was itself inspired by white nationalist rhetoric, efforts, and validations here in the United States. The attack traumatized New Zealand and preoccupied much of the world with yet another sign of the unimpeded rise in dangerous racist animus.

As a Christian, I admit I am sometimes underwhelmed by the church's response to moments like the one in New Zealand. Many Christian denominations immediately offered thoughtful and earnest public denunciations of the violence, as well as expressions of genuine concern for the victims of that tragedy. Truth be told, however, those kinds of statements often strike my ear as innocuous, expressing genuine sorrow but failing to adequately capture the anger many of us feel when confronted with senseless violence. "Our hearts go out to our Muslim sisters and brothers." "We must put an end to the violence." Is this all Christians can say?

Some Christians may find it particularly difficult to say anything compelling in these kinds of situations because they spend too much time in
close proximity to the hate that fuels acts of violence. Specifically, too much
of evangelicalism is at a disadvantage to respond adequately to tragedies like
this one because of the complicity of many evangelical leaders in this kind of
hatred and violence. Every time an evangelical leader says Islam is a violent
and devilish religion and a threat to "Christian America," he stokes animus
toward Islam and dehumanizes the billions of people who identify peace-
fully with that historic tradition. Evangelicalism provides religious cover for
white nationalism when it collapses racial ignorance and jealous patriotism
into religious identity. It harbors nationalists when it provides ideological
justification and political support for demagogues who peddle in racist
dog whistles, absurdly claiming these leaders were sent by God to lead our
nation back to righteousness.[1] Evangelicalism harbors white nationalism
when it refuses to unequivocally reject racism, anti-Semitism, and hatred of
Islam as antithetical to the gospel.

Now in no way is this an accurate description of all evangelicals or
evangelical churches. As a child of evangelical Christianity, I know millions
of American evangelicals faithfully witness to the gospel of love at the heart
of the Way of Jesus and extend that love to sisters and brothers who do not
share their religion. That flavor of evangelicalism was personified in Billy
Graham. While not perfect, Graham offered a Christian ministry that was
deliberately nonpartisan, open to working with Christians along the theological spectrum, racially integrated (if not sufficiently vocal about it), and
(with some embarrassing exceptions in the Nixon era) respectful to other
faiths. Billy Graham understood and preached faith in the saving grace of
Christ lived out in inclusive love of others. By contrast, his son, Franklin
Graham, has made a name for himself by dismantling his father's moral
legacy. As Stephen Prothero wrote in *Politico*, "Franklin Graham is a very
different sort of man" than his father. "Shortly after 9/11, Franklin Graham
provided *the* sound bite of today's culture wars when he denounced Islam as
a 'very wicked and evil religion.' He later became the standard bearer for the
view that Islam is, in his words, 'a religion of hatred . . . a religion of war.'"[2]
My evangelical roots, especially the influence of Billy Graham on my own
faith formation, continue to shape my theology long after I have ceased to
identify with evangelical piety, and I know many other family members and
friends who exhibit the best of evangelicalism. But Franklin Graham and

1. For example, Energy Secretary Rick Perry famously declared that President
Trump was God's "chosen one" to accomplish "great things" in God's name. See Haltiwanger, "Energy Secretary Rick Perry."

2. Prothero, "Billy Graham Built a Movement."

too many current evangelical leaders prize the publicity and political connections that their anti-Muslim rhetoric brings them in this polarized time.

Lest we who identify as liberal Christians feel the impulse to congratu-
late ourselves for being on the enlightened side of our tradition, however,
I should quickly say I also am underwhelmed by the response of mainline
churches to stories of senseless violence. So much of liberal Protestantism
still seems intent on defining its brand of Christianity as generically as possible, standing for little that is distinctive and rendering us liberal Christians
incapable of saying anything helpful in the face of public violence. Allergic
to any kind of commitments that would resemble concrete theological doctrines, we peddle in platitudes of love and justice that add little to the public
response. Can we say nothing more than "Can't we all get along?"

I was angry about what happened in New Zealand. I am angry with the
normalization of hate at a time in American history when we should be celebrating racial and interfaith progress. I am angry with the co-opting of my
religious tradition to provide ideological cover for inhuman atrocity. I am
angry because I do not see enough anger in well-meaning denominational
statements condemning such violence. Therefore, I want to channel my anger into a call that may fall roughly on some ears. I think we Christians need
to declare war on white nationalism. We need a holy war against hate. This is
our righteous cause, that white nationalism is anathema to Christian belief
and antithetical to everything we know to be good in the God disclosed to
us in Jesus Christ. It is the work of the devil, and we must stamp it out. We
must declare a holy war on white nationalism.

As I say, I anticipate that the language of "holy war" will be off-putting
to many Christians, especially left-leaning, pacifism-loving Christians of
the mainline sort, or frankly any chastened believers aware of the historical legacy of Christian crusades in Western history. These days, Christians
tend to talk more in the language of "just war theory," the ethical tradition
of justifying military excursions as a regrettable but sometimes necessary
commitment to violence on behalf of a just cause, like the self-defense of a
nation or the restoration of a people's human rights. The just-war tradition
has given Christians and Western liberalism rich (though not uncontested)
language for identifying circumstances in which war might be justified as
a last resort for accomplishing necessary goals when all other reasonable
options have been exhausted. We greatly prefer to talk of justified wars over
crusades.

Indeed, the language of holy war is politically forbidden in public
discourse over military intervention, because it conjures up the excesses of
medieval crusades, when communities of Muslims, Jews, and even Ortho-
dox Christians were plundered and pillaged with a perverted invocation of

Christ. The idea of a crusade connotes dangerous zealotry and religiously justified mass violence. What makes a crusade is an ideological binary, a belief we are in a battle between good and evil and that the evil must be not only defeated but also annihilated. The us-versus-them extremity of crusading language makes us wary of it, but with all due concern for its bad connotations, the metaphor of a holy war aptly captures my contempt for white nationalism better than the measured reluctance of a just war. I do not think we need a foot-dragging response to white nationalism; we need an enthusiastic engagement. I do not invoke it as a call to violence, but I call it a holy war to signal an ideological call to moral arms, a righteous battle for the gospel of love against the demonic forces of hate. We need a holy war on white nationalism.

We must declare war on white nationalism because it has declared war on us. It has done so by attacking some of the bedrock convictions on which Christianity stands. *White nationalism attacks us when it attacks communities of worshipping Jews and Muslims, because Christians, Muslims, and Jews are theological kin.* Obviously, this is a truth that Christians have struggled to live up to. The church's history of anti-Semitism is brutal. Christian antagonism toward Islam is deep, sometimes met with equal disdain from Muslim extremists. Yet the sacred texts of all three religions remind us we have a shared mythological origin. All three religions trace their lineage to the patriarch Abraham. All three traditions are the stars laid before Abraham as a promise from God and a blessing on the world. Christians, Jews, and Muslims together—in their being—embody God's grace in this world. When Muslims gather for prayer, the world knows that God is great and God is good just as clearly as when Christians gather to sing in their churches. And when pious Muslims are senselessly attacked, that violence is a transgression against God and a wound in the Christian heart. For they are our sisters; they are our brothers. To attack Muslims is to attack the Christian faith.

White nationalism attacks us when it commits acts of violence like in New Zealand, because that kind of violence is an affront to our Christian conviction that all human beings have value in the eyes of God. Martin Luther King Jr. taught us well on this point: every human being is the *imago Dei*, the image of God, the reflection of divine personality in the world. As a result, every human being has value, every human being is inviolable. This is a fundamental tenet of Christian faith; it is the lesson taught in that historic Christian doctrine of incarnation, that in the person of Jesus Christ, God so endorsed human beings as to make it abundantly clear that each of us has value in the eyes of God. When white nationalists attack people of other faiths or people of color, they declare their victims to be less than human, a devaluation of others that Christianity rejects.

White nationalists are a threat to Christianity because the hate they espouse is nothing short of heresy. The language of heresy does not sit well with many Christians of a liberal stripe, because we are convinced liberal Christianity requires us to be allergic to dogmatic litmus tests and parameters for who counts as a Christian. But this may be one of those times when we want to keep in our pocket the prerogative to say there are in fact boundaries on what it means to belong to the Christian fold. There are beliefs that are beyond the acceptable range in the church, so even liberal Christians might want to reserve the right to call something heresy. Hate is a Christian heresy. Hate is antithetical to everything we know about God in the revelation of Christ. Hate is the opposite of love, justice, respect, and regard for other human beings. Hate is the opposite of the ethic by which Jesus lived, that he taught, that he expressed in his death, and that was vindicated in his resurrection. Hate is anti-Christ. Hate in God's name is blasphemous, and we Christians must reject it in no uncertain terms.

Finally, white nationalists attack us when they attack Jews, Muslims, and other religious and racial communities because when they hurt those who are vulnerable, they wound Christ. Jesus could not have been clearer when he taught that all human suffering is an affront to God, and God is present in all human suffering. When we feed the hungry and provide for the thirsty, when we shelter the cold and welcome the stranger, when we mitigate the suffering of those around us, we minister to Jesus himself (Matt 25). By contrast, when we ignore the hungry and thirsty, when we shut up the imprisoned and forget about them, when we round up the stranger, separate them from their children, stoke fear of them, and build walls to keep them away from us, when we prey upon the pious and murder them while they pay homage to God—when we do these things, we do them to Jesus himself. And truly I tell you, says Jesus, those who do these things "will go away into eternal punishment" (Matt 25:46), fuel for the devil and his angels. Human suffering is an affront to God, and God is in all human suffering. The suffering, here and abroad, that results from the hate of white nationalism is an attack on the God we worship and the Christ to whom we pledge allegiance.

So let us declare a holy war on white nationalism. Again, by calling for war I am not suggesting violence against white nationalists. In her work against racism, theologian Kelly Brown Douglas makes clear that the Christian struggle against violence is a battle between the God of life and freedom and the demonic powers of hate:

> The cross . . . represents the consuming violence of the world. It
> points to a world that is saturated with violence. This violence
> includes not simply the physical brutality meant to harm bod-
> ies, but also the systems, structures, narratives, and constructs
> that do harm. Anything that would devalue the life of another is
> violent. God enters into this world of violence, yet God does not
> take it into God's self. Thus, God responds to the violence of the
> world not in an eye-for-an-eye manner. Instead, God responds
> in a way that negates and denounces the violence that demeans
> the integrity of human creation. Thus, through the resurrection,
> God responds to the violence of the cross—the violence of the
> world—in a nonviolent but forceful manner.[3]

The weapons of life and freedom are different than the weapons of
hate. Hate peddles in fear and violence. The God of life assaults with love
and embrace, and as Brown Douglas suggests, in doing so "the forces of
nonviolence actually reveal the impotence of violent power."

Dr. King also called us to respond to violence with soul force, to assert
the dignity of every human being, to stand behind the shield of faith and
wield the sword of love, to do the hard work of even loving those who hate.
We commit to responding to hate with love because of the species of love to
which Christians subscribe, *agape*:

> An overflowing love which seeks nothing in return, *agape* is the
> love of God operating in the human heart. At this level, we love
> men not because we like them, nor because their ways appeal to
> us, nor even because they possess some type of divine spark; we
> love every man because God loves him. At this level, we love the
> person who does an evil deed, although we hate the deed that
> he does.[4]

The weapon of choice for the Christian crusade against hate is this
kind of *agape* love. Violence is not the answer, but redemptive love does get
angry, righteously angry in its hatred of the deeds that white nationalism
perpetrates. White nationalism is the antithesis of all that we stand for as
Christians; it is anathema and heresy. For that reason, racial hatred needs
more than rhetorical response. It needs to be rooted out, confronted, and
destroyed in the cauterizing heat of *agape* love. The first place we ought to
start is its infiltration in our churches.

To come to the spirited defense of the victims of white nationalism does
not require liberal-leaning Christians to apologize for the particularities of

3. Douglas, *Stand Your Ground*, 184.
4. King, *Strength to Love*, 52.

our beliefs or to peddle in generic platitudes. The tragedy inflicted on our sisters and brothers in New Zealand, the mind-boggling hate in Charlottesville, the racist power struggles at our southern border—all of these incidents when white nationalism flexes require us to flex back, with the strength of Christian conviction to say this is not right, this is not normal, this is not who we are, and in the name of God we shall not stand for this anymore. *Salam, Shalom,* and Amen.

21

All the Good Theology
Comes from the Balcony

In my church, all the good theology comes from the balcony. To be clear, both of the Middlebury Congregational Church's pastors are skilled preachers, and each week they share with us inspired interpretations of Christian faith and responsibility. Besides the formal pastors, several others of us take a turn in the pulpit from time to time, and the plurality of voices adds a richness and depth to our community's active discernment of God's presence and intentions. Over the years, however, I have become convinced the most consistently compelling theological utterance in our Sunday worship comes from the balcony, where my good friends Jessica Allen and Jeff Buettner masterfully lead our church choir and play the organ. In the preludes, postludes, introits, and anthems that cascade from the balcony each Lord's Day, our congregation is blessed with a weekly encounter with the divine.

John Calvin once defined the true church as being "wherever we see the Word of God purely preached and heard, and the sacraments administered according to Christ's institution."[1] To my knowledge, he never said

1. Calvin, *Institutes*, 1023.

anything about church requiring a prelude or an anthem for theological authenticity, but I contend that where there is no music, there is likely no church to be found. For one thing, in most mainline Protestant churches no one would show up for a service without music. More importantly, something profoundly theological is lost when music is absent from Christian worship. Although Calvinists have a historic reputation for enmity toward anything aesthetic, and Calvin himself limited the incorporation of music in worship to psalm-singing, I like to think Master Calvin would agree with me about the importance of music, given that church music can serve as a medium by which the "Word of God is preached and heard." Classical church composers like Thomas Tallis and Johann Sebastian Bach often used biblical passages as the springboard for their creations. Standard hymns convey theological themes, like God's steadfast love ("Amazing Grace"), the sufficiency of Christ ("The Church's One Foundation"), the universality of the church ("In Christ There Is No East or West"), or the great commandments as Christian ethic ("They Will Know We Are Christians by Our Love"). In familiar words and tunes, our congregations rehearse who we are and what we believe. The word of God is preached and heard.

Bach is a favorite in our church. Robert Schumann is reported to have said of Bach, "Music owes as much to Bach as religion to its founder."[2] I think religion owes Bach quite a debt too, for it is hard for me to imagine Christian worship without him. Bach was easily one of the five greatest composers in Western music, but he also was one of the most important religious musicians in Christian history. As beautifully illustrated in his *Passion of St. Matthew* and that of *St. John*, Bach considered theology essential to the meaning in his greatest pieces, and many of the hymns, anthems, and organ pieces we cherish in our worship are either his compositions or variations on his themes. Music was theology for Bach, "a harmonious euphony to the Glory of God."[3] If you are like me, there simply is no better way to encounter God's glory than to listen to a little Bach.

In my congregation, however, you are just as likely to hear African-American spirituals, evangelical praise hymns, hits by Bruno Mars, ballads by Bob Dylan, protest songs by Pete Seeger (a local favorite), English carols, Wesleyan hymns, and even the occasional John Denver tune. As a congregation that enjoys a wide range of musical genres, we are not unique, of course. In the cacophony of musical praise we are likely to encounter in church, we can hear genuine God-talk: lyrical professions of faith, Christian identity,

---

2. Goulding, *Classical Music*, 96.
3. Goulding, *Classical Music*, 99.

and moral responsibility that shape our communities of faith and prepare us for faithfulness in the moments in which we live.

Music can be a deeply theological experience because music vividly represents God's beauty and magnificence to us. The last great Puritan, Jonathan Edwards, once wrote "all the beauty to be found throughout the whole creation, is but the reflection of the diffused beams of that Being who hath an infinite fullness of brightness and glory."[4] If Edwards was right, then it is no surprise the reflection of beauty in music often stirs our souls to the point where we would swear we had an encounter with the divine. Music is a gift from God and an opportunity for ecstatic epiphany. It flirts with us in the aesthetic pleasure of the predictable as well as through the inversion of conventions. An intricate postlude testifies to the order and elegance in something seemingly chaotic, as it tests the dexterity of the organist who dares to play it. A comparatively straightforward anthem lifts our hearts with progressions we anticipate though they still move us. Music invites us to soar to new imaginative heights, and evocatively conveys our experience of life's lows. Music reminds us that life, love, tragedy, and loss are all beautiful. It reminds us of the bittersweet in the human experience while giving us glimpses of something more transcendent than our present mendacity. On Easter Sunday in my church, we might utter the phrase "Christ is risen!" no fewer than a half-dozen times in spoken words, but when the choir hits the first "Hallelujah!" from Handel's glorious *Messiah*, that is when most of us become poignantly aware of the presence of the risen Christ in our midst.

An encounter with transcendent beauty is not confined to liturgical music, of course. As I have said already, my church's musical program is as likely to dip into folk tunes and pop favorites as it is to utilize classic Christian hymns. We happily co-opt so-called secular tunes if the words speak to themes compatible with our vision of the Christian life, like love, justice, and reliable kinship. Often, however, music can speak theologically to us regardless of the words, because the music itself is beautiful. My favorite singer, Chris Cornell, allegedly had a four-octave vocal range, and every time I listen to a song in which he pushed the limits of that range, I cannot help but be overcome with a sense of the wonder of God. A voice as awe-inspiring as Cornell's is nothing short of a gift from God, whether or not the words it sings are explicitly pious. When music is beautiful, it testifies to the One who is the source of all beauty. Chris Cornell has yet to make an appearance in our congregation's repertoire, but perhaps one day I will ask to rectify that, because his music is profoundly beautiful, and in its beauty it discloses something of the glory of God.

4. Edwards, *Nature of True Virtue*, 550.

Besides beauty, music helps to convey the unity of Christ's wonderfully diverse church. Music testifies to the great blessing of church because it connects us more effectively than anything else with the church of every time and place. A lot of the music we sing in church today is the same as Christians sang centuries ago. Some of the music we sing comes from Christians worshipping in faraway places. Whether it is bridging time or space, music ties us to the larger church. When we hear a medieval chant, it gathers us in prayer with Christians who lived a millennium or more ago. When we sing a portly German hymn, we are transported back in communion with the faithful in Reformation Europe. When we sing African-American spirituals, we embrace solidarity with kin in cotton fields singing to escape the terrorism that defined their lives. A Latin American hymn whose tempo some of us can barely match, or a Korean hymn with words that tax many American Protestant tongues, reminds us that Christ's church is made up of all kinds of people who do not look, sound, or think exactly like us. Music reminds us of that diversity in the church of every time and place, and it gives us one more reason to offer grateful praise.

Music can connect us not just to places we have never been but to communities we used to know. I grew up in a small Presbyterian church in western Pennsylvania, where my mother served as minister of music for most of my childhood. For several periods in my childhood, our small church was without a preacher, and especially in those days the music program sustained us as a church community and enriched our worship and Christian education. Whether she was playing for Sunday worship, planning one of our regular fellowship nights, or programming the annual Vacation Bible School commencement, my mother made sure music was the centerpiece of our congregation's life together. The music of my childhood church had a simple authenticity that continues to ground me whenever I hear it. I now live in a very different cultural context, and my theology is very different from the evangelicalism in which I was raised. Nonetheless, to this day whenever I hear gospel bluegrass, I recall that community of faith of my youth and their investment in the formation of the "little preacher" in their midst. When I hear one of those old-time hymns that are disappearing from mainline hymnals, or a VBS tune that straightforwardly tells stories of miracles, I think of my mother and her operating principle for church: good music is theological, and good theology is musical.

When we sing songs from long-ago eras or faraway places, we make ourselves available to be transported into deeper communion with enclaves of Christian friends. Music invites us to be less preoccupied with the things that distract and divide us from other Christians than we tend to be when we share spoken words. The liberal New England Congregationalists with whom I worship, for example, seem more tolerant of religious traditionalism in music than they are when the same theological concepts are offered in the form of a sermon or (heaven forbid!) an ancient creed. They are less likely to object to the theology in a Bach chorale or a nineteenth-century spiritual than they would to spoken reference to the same concepts, like resurrection or the Trinity (two ideas that cause consternation for some friends in my church). For good or for bad, we even seem less bothered by gendered references to God in music than we are in speech, and in fact many of my equally progressive friends share my irritation with over-eager hymnal editors who take it upon themselves to cleanse the words of our favorite hymns of male pronouns and antiquated images. The tolerance we show different musical traditions is an indication of music's helpfulness as theological ambassador, translating ideas and perspectives across time and place and enabling us to appreciate (and connect with) differences that have always been characteristic of the body of Christ. In this function as translator, music simply permits the church to be true to its diverse and universal self.

Music is the natural language of a diverse church because it reminds us that Christian faith is fundamentally a poetic experience. Theology is the church's collective project of giving utterance to the experience of God among us and in the world, and poetry captures the diverse and affective nature of those experiences better than propositions. In the post-Scopes trial American church, many liberal and conservative Christians insist on debating the truth of Christianity in propositions. Conservatives define Christianity's truth by flat appeals to inerrant and unchangeable authority, while liberals identify truth by hyper-rational appeals to science. Frankly, I have grown tired of the fundamentalist binary that so much of American Protestantism insists on in its theological title-fights. Neither side possesses adequate creativity to capture the nuance in the relationship between ancient convictions and modern realities.

But poetry revels in nuance and ambiguity, as does music. Poetry seamlessly moves through the disconnect between past and present, as does music. Poetry and music remind us that in the grander scheme of Christian faith and history, "literally true" and "never true" are seldom our only two options. They remind us Christianity is not propositional in its genetic code, despite generations of theologians trying to convince us to the contrary. When done well, Christian theology is not in the business of making empirical claims; instead it simply tries to utter something authentic about the experience of God in our lives, with an unapologetic imprecision that is humanity's only recourse. Theology sheds light on the profundity in our experiences and invites us to imagine Something More than the mundane that surrounds us. When the church does theology, it attempts to capture a bit of God's truth through "symbols, images, ideas, and patterns."[5] It speaks, or perhaps sings, that which cannot be fully explained in words; it gives halting, contextual, and humbly revisable utterance to the wonder of God in the world and in ourselves. When done well, theology is always more poetic than propositional.

Music reminds us that poetry is the church's native language. Poetry and music are especially suited to convey mystical encounters with God and mysteries that defy understanding. Poetry and music therefore invite us to nurture our theological imaginations, to invoke powers and hopes we cannot presently see, to dream of worlds different than the ones we see around us, and to crave the triumph of values different than the ones that prevail in our time and place. Aspiration, inspiration, and imagination are the strengths of poetry, and music captures these poetic impulses in movement, that we might give powerful witness to Christian dissatisfaction with the present and hope for a more grace-filled future.

The Protestant Reformer Martin Luther, author of the classic hymn "A Mighty Fortress Is Our God" and an important contributor to the Protestant musical tradition, once wrote:

> I truly desire that all Christians would love and regard as worthy the lovely gift of music, which is a precious, worthy, and costly treasure given to mankind by God . . . We marvel when we hear music in which one voice sings a simple melody, while three, four, or five other voices play and trip lustily around the voice that sings its simple melody and adorn this simple melody wonderfully with artistic musical effects, thus reminding us of a heavenly dance, where all meet in a spirit of friendliness, caress and embrace.[6]

If theology is poetry, then music is theological verse put to rhythm, a heavenly dance that allows us to feel the presence of God as we move in time with partners we discover in God's name. Better than the spoken word, music captures the soul of Christian theology. It stirs us with God's beauty and majesty, connecting us with spiritual kin in very different times and places and overwhelming us with the reality that we are part of a gorgeously complicated faith family. The experience of music invites us to stretch our

5. See Ottati, *Hopeful Realism*, 26.

6. Luther, Foreword to Georg Rhau (1488–1548), *Symphoniae iucundae*, 324. True to form, Luther could not leave it at that, but instead had to end with his infamous vulgarity and intolerance: "A person who gives this some thought and yet does not regard music as a marvelous creation of God, must be a clodhopper indeed and does not deserve to be called a human being; he should be permitted to hear nothing but the braying of asses and the grunting of hogs."

imaginations, that we might draw faith, hope, and love not just from what is seen but from what is unseen. Good music makes us theological, and good theology makes us musical. For these reasons, and with all due respect to the importance of the pulpit, I am convinced the best theology often comes from the balcony.

22

The Sacred in the Profane

Allow me a confession: I have a potty mouth. My propensity to swear, in private and increasingly in public, is a habit that has grown as I have evolved from an excessively righteous twenty-something to a middle-aged Generation Xer resigned to many of his shortcomings. I curse more than I did back then, and with decreasing concern for context. My classroom vernacular is certainly less pristine than it was when I was a newly minted PhD, and sometime after the toddler years I lost the energy to filter my language in front of my children. Now I seem intent on ensuring my boys are never surprised on the school bus, for they are unlikely to encounter a colorful word there that they did not first learn from the mouth of their father. Even my dogs know the profane vocabulary, cues for when it is time to help neutralize my temper or simply leave the room.

I swear for several reasons. Most often I swear because I am angry, and I am frequently angry. I have inherited a temper that runs deep in the family lineage, and swearing serves as an expression of anger as well as a pressure release, preferred over some of the other options men in my family have employed (like throwing things and, as the legends of Pap-Pap tell it, running to the closet for a handy shotgun). Swearing helps me channel anger's physiological energy verbally rather than physically, although a law of diminishing returns applies, so that the more I use certain words the less effective they are for mood recovery. As a result, I find myself having to reach for more vivid and less acceptable alternatives to assuage my need for therapy. If my temper fails to plateau with age, I may need to start making up new words of my own.

Anger is not the only reason I swear. Sometimes I do it just for fun. I once read an interview with Christian music artist Amy Grant, where she too admitted that she occasionally liked to go a little blue, just for the shock value of it.[1] Amy Grant is much more wholesome than I am, so I figure if it is acceptable to her it must be fine for me. Colorful language is funny, because it can insert a surprise into an otherwise dull conversation. Sometimes it encourages creativity; it can augment the description of an event or person to make a story, characterization, or complaint more "vivid." Profanity is especially fun when it travels in the company of its rhetorical sibling, crudity. My brother is one of my favorite people in the world, because he is the one person (besides my spouse) with whom I feel I can be totally and honestly me. He does not relate to me as clergy, writer, or college professor, but as family, and part of our fraternal dynamic always has been a rather disgusting brand of humor. When I am home visiting, we regularly engage in verbal contests to see which one of us can gross out the other, and when he taps out and leaves my mother's kitchen table, I am left with an unsurpassed feeling of satisfaction.

The role of profanity and crude humor in the bond I share with my brother speaks to another reason I swear, as an expression of class and cultural identity. I am the son and grandson of Appalachian coal miners, and that heritage remains an important part of who I am, even if (or especially because) I no longer live in the blue-collar milieu of western Pennsylvania. Solidly ensconced in the upper-middle class and surrounded by other white-collar professionals, I am desperate to hold on to some part of my hillbilly upbringing. Anthropologists tell us culture is perpetuated by rituals and traditions, and I hold on to my native culture by living in the country, riding a motorcycle, rocking tattoos, listening to bluegrass music, and swearing. Not everyone in my home community used profanity, but lots of people did, for it was working-class vernacular, signaling a rough-around-the-edges-because-we-have-to-be attitude. For me the use of profanity reminds me of my roots, as well as the character and concerns that accompany life in the working class.[2]

1. Jahr, "Amy Grant."

2. Christian ethicist Stanley Hauerwas, who for years was known for his liberal use of profanity in all kinds of academic and ecclesial circles (including meetings of the Society of Christian Ethics, where I encountered it firsthand), offers a similar explanation

Whether as an outlet to anger, an expression of culture, or just a recreational hobby, I use profanity somewhat liberally, and it might come as a surprise to hear a preacher and theologian admit that with little remorse. People who know me primarily in the context of Christian faith might be scandalized to discover the shadowy side to my vocabulary, and indeed I used to worry about running into a church friend while letting loose a string of blue over a broken bag in the supermarket parking lot. These days I worry less, mostly because I am older and do not care as much about what people think of me, but also because my closest friends currently are a congregation of people who embrace me for who I am. They already know that my clerical model is more the Clint Eastwood character from *Pale Rider* than it is Mister Rogers, so they are unlikely to be surprised by what comes out of my mouth. Indeed, some of them probably love me more for it.

Still, profanity does not seem a very pious habit, according to many Christians. The common conviction that profanity is incompatible with Christian living normally finds root in a reading of the Ten Commandments: "Thou shalt not take the name of the Lord thy God in vain" (Exod 20:7 KJV). We often take that commandment as a prohibition on cursing, but in fact it says little to nothing about what we consider profanity today. The commandment demands respect for the honor of God's name, which was at risk when God's name was employed in frivolous oaths, literal curses, and contests with charlatans of rival gods. The recreational or therapeutic profanity of which I am guilty is not really the target of the commandment. Perhaps I still run afoul of it, however, as my ever-widening reservoir of swear words includes options that begin with g-o-d. In my defense, the first of those letters is intentionally lower case when I use the offending terms, which clearly signals my intention to direct disrespect only to the false gods out there in the world, not to the great I AM. I am pretty sure God hears the distinction, since the Bible assures us that God knows the things we utter in secret (Matt 5:6), whether they be sacred or profane.

To be honest, the picture of a God totally preoccupied with affronts to divine honor is a depiction of the holy that made more sense in ancient cultures than it does (at least to me) today. I prefer to think God is not as pettily offended as we are, that God is more concerned with how we

---

for his language choice. Hauerwas claims he swore because that is how the son of a bricklayer was taught to speak, and to do so was to push back on "the middle-class and upper-middle-class etiquette that dominated university life" and that he found "oppressive." Hauerwas insinuated he used profane language in academic settings as a deliberate effort to provoke, and he only ceased doing so when he "became tired of and bored with having that aspect of my life made into such a 'big deal'" (Hauerwas, *Hannah's Child*, 120). As a fellow son of the working class now similarly trapped in very different cultural circumstances, Hauerwas's justification makes perfect sense to me.

treat one another than with perceived verbal slights to God's holy name. Of course, plenty of Christians still think the inappropriate use of God's name is at the top of God's concerns, and this conviction represents the rare rift between President Trump and his legion of evangelical devotees. As is evident to anyone who watches the news, the president regularly stokes his supporters by talking in ugly fashion about his perceived enemies. He has a long history of disparaging minorities, ridiculing people with disabilities, demeaning women, and assigning nicknames to his political nemeses like a schoolyard bully. None of this behavior has dampened his support among evangelical Christians, but evangelical leaders have openly objected to his tendency to take the Lord's name in vain. They are willing to ignore or perhaps implicitly endorse his misogyny, racism, disdain for the vulnerable, and general meanness, but please, Mr. President, stop saying "g*ddamn."[3]

Unlike some of those self-appointed spokespersons for American Christendom, I find it unfathomable that God suffers from inordinate preoccupation with that one word in Trump's vocabulary. Christ showed us God's priorities when he warned, "just as you did not do it to one of the least of these, you did not do it to me" (Matt 25:45). Ignoring the hungry, homeless, sick, and stranger were the wounds Christ felt in himself; he said nothing about taking casual curse words as a personal insult. I suspect when God finally arranges a meeting with Donald Trump, taking the Lord's name in vain will be well down the list of things for which God will demand an accounting.

I think our Christian concern with profanity is largely a cultural import, a collapse of popular notions of decorum into our understanding of religious piety. Many Christians today consider swearing a sinful habit because they have come to believe adhering to conventions of politeness are part of what it means to be a good Christian. I worry about the Christian baptism of decorum, though, because enforcement of social norms has been used in the past as a way to neutralize the marginalized in their efforts to exert freedom or legitimacy. Once upon a time, decorum dictated that women be docile, that people of different races not mix, and that people of the same sex not sleep together. At one time or another, Christianity has endorsed each of these conventions of decorum as Christian truth, and for some Christians they still apply as religious mores. From my perspective, however, each of them is an example of cultural injustice dressed up in the garb of religious imperative, oppression made to resemble nondisruptive piety.

3. For more on the consternation Trump's language causes for evangelical leaders, see Zauzmer, "Trump Uttered What Many Supporters Consider Blasphemy."

The collapse of conventions of decorum into Christian faithfulness can reinforce oppressive practices and distract us from what really ought to matter to followers of Jesus Christ. Widespread suffering among the vulnerable is a deeper wound to the ethics of the gospel than the use of blue language. In fact, sometimes profanity can serve the purposes of the gospel, believe it or not, especially when it helps to convey the level of disgust we experience over injustices in our society. In other words, sometimes profanity can convey prophetic anger over social sin better than socially acceptable rhetoric. Popular notions of nicety train us to think anger itself is a bad thing, an emotion to avoid or get over as soon as possible. But as theologian Beverly Harrison taught, anger can serve the work of Christian love by signaling something morally amiss in our relationships or society:

> Anger is a mode of connectedness to others and it is always a vivid form of caring. To put the point another way: anger is—and it always is—a sign of some resistance in ourselves to the moral quality of the social relations in which we are immersed. Extreme and intense anger signals a deep reaction to the action upon us or toward others to whom we are related . . . Anger denied subverts community. Anger expressed directly is a mode of taking the other seriously, of caring.[4]

Sometimes anger is the expression we need to indicate our concern with injustices in our moral community.

Anger over injustice lies at the heart of the prophetic tradition. The anger of the prophet serves as the "moral chemotherapy" (to use Cathleen Kaveny's insightful phrase) necessary for a disordered society to recognize and respond to what ails it.[5] Anger is the shock to the system that allows our collective heart to start beating again. One cannot read the biblical prophets and fail to hear their anger at the abuse of the poor and the outcast and the foreigners in their midst. I wonder if the prophetic literature bequeathed to us in the Bible is a cleaned-up edition of the prophets' words, the "network broadcast" version, so to speak. The "cable version" remains hidden to us, but if Isaiah, Jeremiah, Micah, and the others were as angry over social sin as their words suggest, might they have shown it with more colorful language than the biblical scribes recorded? Is it possible that in real time, one or more of those spokespersons for God's justice dropped the Hebrew equivalent of an F-bomb or two, as the moral chemotherapy their communities needed to see their way back to God? Is

4. Harrison, "Power of Anger in the Work of Love," 14–15.

5. For the description of prophetic discourse as "moral chemotherapy," see Kaveny, *Prophecy without Contempt*, 287.

it possible, for instance, that an "ever-flowing stream" (Amos 5:24) is not the only metaphor Amos employed to make God's cause known to ears that would not hear it?

Anger sometimes contributes to the work of love, and profanity sometimes lends power to our righteous anger. To be honest, however, most of the time I let off a bad word, I do not do so as a commentary on social injustices. Most of the time, I swear because I am mad at something more trivial, or I am entertaining myself. Even in those times, however, I like to think that God is not greatly taxed over my profanity. God has more important things to worry about than my therapeutic or recreational use of forbidden words.

Does all of this mean, then, that Christians should regard swearing as unproblematic, perhaps unambiguously good? Not quite, for there is one Christian argument against swearing I find compelling, so much so that it has inspired me to write this entire essay on profanity without using a single swear word in it. If there is an argument for Christians to temper their use of profanity, at least in public, it is this: "Let us therefore no longer pass judgment on one another, but resolve instead never to put a stumbling block or hindrance in the way of another" (Rom 14:13). Toward the end of his letter to the Romans, Paul reminds his readers of the obligations of love. Members of the same community will hold different convictions about what is appropriate to living out the faith. Some of us may have scruples that others consider unimportant, even wrongheaded. Nonetheless, says Paul, just because you think something is allowable does not mean you should do it. Even if it is permissible, if it is not essential and will cause a fellow Christian concern or harm, refrain from that action in their presence, out of love for your sisters and brothers in Christ. Do not impede the faith of others unnecessarily by causing intentional affront to their sense of what is right and good. "Each of us must please our neighbor for the good purpose of building up the neighbor," advises Paul (Rom 15:2).

The early Roman Christians were preoccupied with concerns over taboo foods and connections with Jewish law, but Paul's advice seems pertinent to our topic too. Even if some of us think profanity is not theologically dubious, that does not mean we should let fly with four-letter words indiscriminately. Many other Christians believe such language is objectionable and incompatible with Christian piety, and the use of profanity may not be important enough a conviction for us to press the point. Better that we watch our language when we are in the company of Christians with such scruples, as an expression of respect for our sisters and brothers in the faith. Building up my neighbor and the shared community of faith is important enough to guard my tongue from time to time.

Sometimes respect for my neighbor is the reason I do not swear, and other times it is the reason I do. Profanity may call strident attention to injustice and prompt us to action. Profanity may lend levity to shared life with others, infusing fun and friendship to balance out hard times. But sometimes profanity may hurt, and in those circumstances respect for my neighbor should cause me to prioritize the building up of others over letting off steam in this particular way. Either way, the God we worship and adore intimately understands the human needs and shortcomings that cause people like me to utter off-color words. We know God understands the challenges of being human because of that ancient Christian doctrine of incarnation, which reminds us that Christ, "though he was in the form of God . . . emptied himself, taking the form of a slave, being born in human likeness" (Phil 2:6–7). In the person of Jesus Christ, we are assured the sacred understands the needs of the profane. I like to believe that includes the need for us to blow off steam every now and then, even if we require the use of language more suitable to the bar than the sanctuary. Given that the incarnate God is also the Creator from whom all things—including humor—come, perhaps God even thinks some of my bad words are funny.

23

The Christian Misanthrope

Can you be a Christian misanthrope? The Merriam-Webster Diction-
ary defines a misanthrope as "a person who hates or distrusts hu-
mankind." Precisely used, the term refers to someone who retreats from
human interaction out of a rejection of human community itself, and so
it is clear that the concept of a Christian misanthrope is an impossibility. The Christian tradition's emphases on love and community make it
hard to identify with Christian faith and completely detach ourselves from
humanity. I ask the question, though, because I have been called a misanthrope from time to time, even though I am quite publicly a Christian. I
assume the charge of being misanthropic is leveled tongue-in-cheek, since
it usually comes from friends, people close to me who know my strong
preference for alone time and independence. The description has been
offered frequently enough, however, that I cannot help but wonder if I am
a walking contradiction in terms.

To call my thirst for solitude a "strong preference" is an understate-
ment. My default is to be alone, and so it requires considerable deliberate
energy for me to seek out the company of other people. I like quiet time
with my own thoughts or even (as Simon and Garfunkel would appreciate)
the sound of silence. A good weekend to me is spent walking in the woods

THE CHRISTIAN MISANTHROPE

behind my house, sitting on my porch staring at the deer in the field across the way, or tinkering with a project in my garage. I often prefer time to talk to myself over talking with others, and I find pointless exchanges (what polite people call "small talk") excruciating endurance tests. When I underwent psychological evaluation during the process of preparing for ordained ministry, the tests concluded that if I were any more introverted, I would simply be dead, much to the consternation of the committee shepherding me to ordination. At the college where I teach, we have a custom of beginning the academic year with a massive party for staff and faculty, hosted by the president. In twenty years at my institution, I have not darkened the door of that festival, not even once. A colonoscopy seems a more comfortable and less intrusive way to spend an evening.

Yes, I have been called a misanthrope, and it is tempting to conclude the label fits, except I do not actually dislike people. I do not like crowds and I am allergic to most social occasions, but I love people. I especially love spending quality time with people of whom I am fond, in small numbers and intentional engagements. I genuinely enjoy running into certain colleagues at work, and I relish my interaction with friends at church. In the case of a handful of very special friends, I actually hunger to see them between our visits. My default in life, however, is to be alone, for that is when I truly relax and recharge my mental and emotional batteries. Friendships are welcomed interruptions to a predominantly solitary life, not the other way around.

I am a preacher and teacher, of course, and many people who know me from those public and performative roles declare confidently that I cannot possibly be as introverted as I claim. "You are so comfortable in front of crowds," they say. "You are so confident in public settings and leadership roles. You are not shy!" But shyness and introversion are not the same thing. I can rise to the occasion and channel my energy to teach and preach, and I even find joy and considerable meaning in those roles. But performance in those roles is just that—public service, and the fulfillment of speaking or teaching duties comes at a personal cost. Social interaction drains me, so that each occasion of public performance must be followed by a lengthy opportunity to refuel, alone. In the two or three hours after worship, I do little more than stare into space in a moment of quiet or sit and watch football with my family. After class, I immediately retreat to my office for a safer, quieter exercise, like reading the news or catching up on email. I am hardwired to need a lot of alone time to be well.

Being a private person or craving solitude does not itself make you a misanthrope. A misanthrope does not like being around people, does not even like them, but introverts like me can love people and still need our interpersonal engagements to come in small, chewable doses. Even if that does not make me a misanthrope, though, does the disinclination to be social make me an inferior Christian? It is easy to think it does, given how much we Christians talk about love and community. Christianity defines "the good life" as living in community, namely the community of the church. We characterize the life of faith as fellowship with others following the Way of Jesus. Some of our most common practices suggest extensive people-time is a fundamental part of being Christian. In the passing of the peace, for instance, we show our commitment to community by working our way around the sanctuary, grabbing the hand and patting the shoulder of as many people as we can reach in the excruciatingly long time allotted to this ritual. A very good church friend of mine (and fellow introvert) is fond of approaching me in worship and declaring "spiritual hug!" as a substitute for the enforced physical expressions of affection that make us both uncomfortable. I suspect her idea of a spiritual hug will become more mainstream as we adjust Christian practices to a post-coronavirus age.

Other common practices seem to define the church as naturally extroverted. In fellowship hours after Sunday worship, we practice faith community by jamming fifty or a hundred people in one room for a massive social encounter. We lift up as quintessential Christian servants those who deftly work a room of relative strangers at a meal or clinic or school. Another idea that gets play in some congregations, especially squishy liberal ones like mine, is standing in a circle and turning to the person next to us to engage them in a short-range exercise of Christian spiritual intimacy. When the extroverts are feeling especially masochistic, one of them will suggest we hold hands while we do it, because the close encounter itself is not excruciating enough. All of these rituals are common ways of being church, but I look forward to none of them, because they ask of me something that I do not naturally possess, an unguarded capacity for the interpersonal. Our intractably sociable church practices sometimes seem incompatible with how I am built. I suspect I am not alone (in fact, I know it), even if my version of introversion is especially clinical. Given our discomfort with these common elements of Christian practice, are we introverted Christians *inferior* Christians?

Honestly, I know I am a decidedly imperfect Christian, but I wonder how much of the disconnect I experience between who I am and what church requires is because being church is so often defined by extroverts. Whether we are talking about church or culture, we introverts have to admit the extroverts have numbers. American culture is dominated by and defined by extroverts, people who get energy from other people and therefore define what is right and good by encounters with other people. A couple years ago, corporate consultant Susan Cain wrote a delightful book called *Quiet: The Power of Introverts in a World That Can't Stop Talking*, in which she observed that popular culture is dominated by the extroverted norm.[1] Her book focuses on business and financial culture, and she points out that extroverts are behind the assumption that talking, teamwork, and networking are essential goods to healthy business and financial success. The marginalization of introverts, she argues, leads to a corresponding devaluation of habits we introverts do better than networking, traits like thoughtfulness, depth, thoroughness, a capacity for listening, and a priority on creative independence. Cain argues persuasively that the financial crisis of 2008 may not have happened if a few more introverts were contributing to Wall Street culture, infusing the financial sector with their characteristic caution, pace, and critical reflection to counterbalance the aggressiveness and impulsiveness that sometimes comes with extroverts.

On the one hand, if you see a bit of yourself in my self-portrait so far, you might want to read Cain's book to reassure yourself you are not alone in the world. On the other hand, if this introverted life seems odd and foreign to you, you still might do all of us introverts a favor and pick up the book, because odds are you could stand to see how the other half lives. What Cain says about popular and business culture is true of church culture too. I think we sometimes collapse Christian virtues into specifically extroverted interpretations of those values, because many churchgoers and church leaders are themselves extroverts. So the Christian priority on neighbor-love is interpreted to necessarily require as much interpersonal connection as the day will hold, evangelism is understood to consist solely of cold-calling strangers about the love of Jesus, and service only counts if we make physical contact with the people we help.

If we think about it, though, we might be able to imagine living out Christian values in more varied form, including practices that better suit those of us who do not naturally live outside of ourselves. Christian service can consist of "impersonal tasks" (like cleaning facilities or doing church mailings) as much as the direct service for which extroverts can be especially suited. Small group fellowship opportunities are a lovely complement to a large fellowship hour, because they provide opportunity to develop meaningful relationships with a few people at a time, at a pace that suits those of us for whom socializing is a high-impact workout. Silent prayer makes many extroverts uncomfortable, but it speaks to introverts in its ritualistic endorsement of the value of silence. (Extroverts often self-identify during silent prayer, by moving around after they have decided the silence has gone

1. Cain, *Quiet*.

on an inappropriately long time, usually not more than fifteen seconds. By contrast, most introverts could sit silently through a Quaker meeting without feeling an ounce of discomfort.) For the sake of Christian introverts, it is worth asking whether our church practices are necessary expressions of Christian piety or reflections of a specifically extroverted interpretation of Christian piety. If the latter, could we change up our liturgical and community practices more often than we do?

When I am feeling my most out of stride as a Christian, I like to think of Jesus as an introvert. "Oh," you might say, "Jesus could not have been an introvert. Look at the way he loved people and spent all his documented time in crowds large and small." The Gospels suggest Jesus was a compelling public speaker, not shy or withdrawn. But again, shyness and introversion are not the same thing. Jesus effectively lived into his public role, as we introverts often do, but the Gospels tell us on several occasions Jesus retreated from the public eye into stillness and quiet. From time to time he left his friends and adoring crowds to hide on the other side of a lake, in a wilderness, or in a garden. Of course, the Gospels do not give us play-by-play of his entire adult life, so for all we know Jesus engaged in retreat more than the Bible suggests. Perhaps it was a frequent practice of his to escape public performance to the solitude of his own mind and heart, to care for his interior self and commune with God. Because of what the Gospels tell us about Jesus as well as what they leave out, I think it is entirely appropriate to imagine Jesus as an introvert too.

If the idea of Jesus as introvert is not totally far-fetched, then perhaps we introverts reflect something authentic about the Way of Jesus, and therefore do not have reason to feel like inferior Christians just because we fail to measure up to the social standards of our extroverted church.[2] If that is the case, then perhaps personality diversity is another dimension to a proudly pluralistic Christian communion that we need to more intentionally reflect. The apostle Paul reminds us the church needs its different parts, and that diversity in our ranks is not a problem to solve but a richness we need in order to be church. When we read 1 Corinthians 12, for instance, we usually assume Paul is talking about differences in gifts, skills, and roles when he talks about the different parts of the body of Christ. Sometimes we also read Paul to be reminding us to be generous to people of different convictions within church. Perhaps another way to apply his metaphor of body

2. This contention that introversion and interiority represent an authentic interpretation of Christian piety is justified not just by speculation about the personality of Jesus. We also see interiority reflected as a theological priority in the deep history of Christian spirituality, including Christian poets and mystics like John Chrysostom, Catherine of Siena, Julian of Norwich, Francis of Assisi, and Thomas Merton.

parts, however, is to make room for different *personality types.* Honoring the range of personalities that make up church is another way to affirm the church needs its arms and feet, eyes and ears. We make room in church for the introvert not just by accommodating their social awkwardness, but by embracing them and admitting that their preference for quiet, focus, and selective social engagement is a constructive part of the diversity with which God blesses the body of Christ. Introverts can bring capacities for critical reflection to leadership opportunities, a fondness for quiet to worship planning, and a depth of thoughtfulness to spiritual formation. These gifts helpfully complement the gifts normally associated with extroverts. Like our socially minded extroverts, the church needs its introverted members: "If all were a single member, where would the body be? As it is, there are many members, yet one body" (1 Cor 12:19–20).

What would it look like to honor more faithfully the different personality types that make up the body of Christ? It could mean lifting up the volunteer who sits in an office stuffing envelopes for church or charity as practicing laudable Christian service just as valiantly as the one who serves meals or visits the sick, for the envelope stuffers too are doing what they can to serve their community. It could mean thinking about the impact our fellowship opportunities might have on different participants (new and established) in our congregations, including some for whom a deep dive into a mass of strangers may not come as a welcoming invite. It could mean incorporating more silence into our worship practices, our educational activities, and our meetings from time to time.

While we are doling out sensitivity training for an extroverted church, however, those of us who are introverts also have something to learn from the extroverts in our midst. It is good for us "misanthropes" to be in church with lots of extroverts, for extroverts remind us that in the Christian worldview, living in community is normally not optional. We need people to live the life Christ taught us to live. Some of us need to balance our social interactions with alone time more intentionally than others, but you cannot be a Christian in isolation. I know, because I have tried it.

If the COVID-19 pandemic has taught us anything, it is that both the project of being human and the privilege of being church require community to feel whole and healthy. Sheltering in place was an experiment in extreme isolation, and for many Americans it did not go well. We were reminded we need regular interactions with other people to be fully human, even those of us with an extensive appetite for solitude. Those interactions need to be full and embodied to be truly human; virtual visits can get us through a global crisis, but long-term they will not sustain us. Similarly, the life of faith cannot be authentic when we try to live it without others. The

Christian covenant with God has never been an exclusive relationship; it always involves experiencing God and obeying God through our experience of and obligations to other people. The Christian life, like the human project to which it testifies, is a life lived with others. A zealous misanthrope cannot faithfully discharge the duties of discipleship if she insists on catering solely to the needs of the interior life. An extroverted church, with its embodiment of Christian love, friendship, and community reminds us introverts that the Way of Jesus was meant to be traveled with company, at least some of the time. Extroverted Christians keep introverts like me spiritually honest.

Perhaps the ideal balance for church is captured in one of the central rituals of being church, the sacrament of Communion, especially as many Protestant congregations practice it. For some of our churches, it is regular habit to eat the bread together as a celebration of our bonds to each other in Christ, but then we take the cup separately as an acknowledgment of the ways Christ comes to us as individuals. Both parts of this eucharistic symbolism are profound and faithful. Christ meets us in the faces of those to our right and our left, in the embrace of a beloved neighbor, and in the outreached hand of a stranger. Christ also meets us in the solitary, silent, mystical moments of our lives, when we are truly and completely alone.

Bibliography

Achtemeier, Mark. *The Bible's Yes to Same-Sex Marriage: An Evangelical's Change of Heart.* Louisville: Westminster John Knox, 2014.

Aristotle. *The Nicomachean Ethics.* New York: Penguin Classics, 2004.

Augustine. "The Good of Marriage." In *Theology and Sexuality: Classic and Contemporary Readings,* edited by Eugene F. Rogers, 71–86. Malden, MA: Blackwell, 2002.

Bradford, William. *Of Plymouth Plantation, 1620–1647.* New York: The Modern Library, 1981.

"A Brief Statement of Faith." In *The Constitution of the Presbyterian Church (U.S.A.),* Part I, *Book of Confessions.* Louisville: Office of the General Assembly, Presbyterian Church (U.S.A.), 2016.

Brueggemann, Walter. *Sabbath as Resistance: Saying No to the Culture of Now.* Rev. ed. Louisville: Westminster John Knox, 2017.

Cahill, Lisa Sowle. *Love Your Enemies: Discipleship, Pacifism, and Just War Theory.* Minneapolis: Augsburg Fortress, 1997.

Cain, Susan. *Quiet: The Power of Introverts in a World That Can't Stop Talking.* New York: Broadway, 2013.

Calvin, John. *Institutes of the Christian Religion.* Edited by John T. McNeil. Philadelphia: Westminster, 1960.

Coffin, William Sloane. "Alex's Death." In *A Chorus of Witnesses: Model Sermons for Today's Preachers,* edited by Thomas G. Long and Cornelius Plantinga, Jr., 262–66. Grand Rapids: Eerdmans, 1994.

Cone, James H. *The Cross and the Lynching Tree.* Maryknoll, NY: Orbis, 2011.

Culp, Kristine A. "Always Reforming, Always Resisting." In *Feminist and Womanist Essays in Reformed Dogmatics,* edited by Amy Plantinga Pauw and Serene Jones, 152–68. Louisville: Westminster John Knox, 2006.

Daly, Mary. *Beyond God the Father: Toward a Philosophy of Women's Liberation.* Rev. ed. Boston: Beacon, 2015.

Davis, James Calvin. *Forbearance: A Theological Ethic for a Disagreeable Church.* Grand Rapids: Eerdmans, 2017.

————. *In Defense of Civility: How Religion Can Unite America on Seven Moral Issues That Divide Us.* Louisville: Westminster John Knox, 2010.

Dawkins, Richard. *The God Delusion.* London: Bantam, 2006.

Dorrien, Gary. *The Making of American Liberal Theology.* 3 vols. Louisville: Westminster John Knox, 2001, 2003, 2006.

————. *Social Ethics in the Making: Interpreting an American Tradition.* West Sussex: Wiley-Blackwell, 2011.

Douglas, Kelly Brown. *Stand Your Ground: Black Bodies and the Justice of God.* Maryknoll, NY: Orbis, 2015.

Edwards, Jonathan. *The Nature of True Virtue.* In *The Works of Jonathan Edwards*, vol. 5, edited by Paul Ramsey, 537–627. 26 vols. New Haven: Yale University Press, 1989.

Farley, Margaret A. *Just Love: A Framework for Christian Sexual Ethics.* New York: Continuum, 2006.

Federal Council of Churches, "The Social Creed of the Churches." https://national councilofchurches.us/common-witness/1908/social-creed.php.

Fiorenza, Elisabeth Schussler. *In Memory of Her.* New York: Crossroad, 1989.

Frey, William H. "The U.S. Will Become 'Minority White' in 2045, Census Projects." *Brookings*, March 14, 2018. https://www.brookings.edu/blog/the-avenue/2018/03/14/the-us-will-become-minority-white-in-2045-census-projects/.

Goulding, Phil G. *Classical Music: The 50 Greatest Composers and Their 1000 Greatest Works.* New York: Fawcett Columbine, 1992.

Green, Clifford, ed. *Karl Barth: Theologian of Freedom.* Philadelphia: Fortress, 1991.

Gustafson, James M. *Ethics from a Theocentric Perspective.* 2 vols. Chicago: University of Chicago Press, 1983, 1984.

Guthrie, Shirley. *Christian Doctrine.* Rev. ed. Louisville: Westminster John Knox, 1994.

Haltiwanger, John. "Energy Secretary Rick Perry in a Fox News Interview Called Trump 'The Chosen One' Who Was 'Sent by God to Do Great Things.'" *Business Insider*, November 25, 2019. https://www.businessinsider.com/rick-perry-fox-news-trump-chosen-one-sent-by-god-2019–11.

Harrison, Beverly Wildung. "The Power of Anger in the Work of Love: Christian Ethics for Women and Other Strangers." In *Making the Connections: Essays in Feminist Social Ethics*, edited by Carol S. Robb, 3–21. Boston: Beacon, 1985.

Hauerwas, Stanley. *Hannah's Child: A Theologian's Memoir.* Grand Rapids: Eerdmans, 2010.

Hauerwas, Stanley, and William H. Willimon. *Resident Aliens: A Provocative Assessment of Culture and Ministry for People Who Know Something Is Wrong.* Nashville: Abingdon, 1989.

Holley, Peter. "Pat Robertson Says Halloween Is the Day When 'Millions of Children . . . Celebrate Satan.'" *Washington Post*, October 31, 2015. https://www.washingtonpost.com/news/acts-of-faith/wp/2015/10/31/pat-robertson-says-halloween-is-the-day-when-millions-of-children-celebrate-satan/.

Jahr, Cliff. "Amy Grant: 'I'm Not a Prude.'" *Ladies Home Journal*, December 1985. https://web.archive.org/web/20051018082843/http://amygrant.offramp.org/info/articles/ung/8.html.

Jones, Robert P. *The End of White Christian America.* New York: Simon & Schuster, 2016.

Kaveny, Cathleen. *Prophecy without Contempt: Religious Discourse in the Public Square.* Cambridge: Harvard University Press, 2016.

Kessler, Glen, et al. "President Trump Made 16,241 False or Misleading Claims in His First Three Years." *Washington Post*, January 20, 2020. https://www.washingtonpost. com/politics/2020/01/20/president-trump-made-16241-false-or-misleading-claims-his-first-three-years/.

King, Martin Luther, Jr. "A Christmas Sermon on Peace." In *A Testament of Hope: The Essential Writings and Speeches of Martin Luther King, Jr.*, edited by James M. Washington, 253–58. New York: HarperCollins, 1986.

———. "I Have a Dream." In *A Testament of Hope: The Essential Writings and Speeches of Martin Luther King, Jr.*, edited by James M. Washington, 217–20. New York: HarperCollins, 1986.

———. *Strength to Love*. Philadelphia: Fortress, 1963.

Langford, Michael J. *The Tradition of Liberal Theology*. Grand Rapids: Eerdmans, 2014.

Luther, Martin. Foreword to Georg Rhau, *Symphoniae iucundae* (1538). In *Luther's Works*, vol. 53, edited by Ulrich S. Leupold, 321–24. 55 vols. Philadelphia: Fortress, 1965.

McFague, Sallie. *Models of God: Theology for an Ecological, Nuclear Age*. Philadelphia: Fortress, 1987.

Mishel, Lawrence, and Julia Wolfe. "CEO Compensation Has Grown 940% since 1978." *Economic Policy Institute Report*, August 14, 2019. https://www.epi.org/ publication/ceo-compensation-2018/.

National Council of Churches. "A 21st Century Creed." https://nationalcouncilofchurches. us/a-21st-century-social-creed.

Niebuhr, H. Richard. *Christ and Culture*. New York: Harper & Row, 1951.

Niebuhr, Reinhold. "Christian Faith and the Race Problem." In *Love and Justice: Selections from the Shorter Writings of Reinhold Niebuhr*, edited by D. B. Robertson, 125–29. Philadelphia: Westminster, 1957.

———. "Democracy as a False Religion." In *Reinhold Niebuhr: Theologian of Public Life*, edited by Larry Rasmussen, 256–58. London: Collins, 1989.

———. *Moral Man and Immoral Society*. New York: Scribners, 1932.

———. "Why the Christian Church Is Not Pacifist." In *Reinhold Niebuhr: Theologian of Public Life*, edited by Larry Rasmussen, 237–53. London: Collins, 1989.

Ottati, Douglas F. *Hopeful Realism: Reclaiming the Poetry of Theology*. Cleveland: Pilgrim, 1999.

———. *Theology for Liberal Protestants: God the Creator*. Grand Rapids: Eerdmans, 2013.

Parini, Jay. *Promised Land: Thirteen Books That Changed America*. New York: Doubleday, 2008.

Prothero, Stephen. "Billy Graham Built a Movement. Now His Son Is Dismantling It." *Politico*, February 24, 2018. https://www.politico.com/magazine/story/2018 /02/24/billy-graham-evangelical-decline-franklin-graham-217077.

Rauschenbusch, Walter. *Christianity and the Social Crisis in the Twenty-First Century: The Classic That Woke Up the Church*. Edited by Paul Rauschenbusch. San Francisco: HarperOne, 2007.

Reich, Robert B. *Aftershock: The Next Economy and America's Future*. New York: Vintage, 2010.

Rogers, Eugene F., ed. *Theology and Sexuality: Classic and Contemporary Readings*. Malden, MA: Blackwell, 2002.

Ryan, John A. *Economic Justice: Selections from* Distributive Justice *and* A Living Wage. Edited by Harlan R. Beckley. Louisville: Westminster John Knox, 1996.

Spong, John Shelby. *Unbelievable: Why Neither Ancient Creeds Nor the Reformation Can Produce a Living Faith Today.* San Francisco: HarperOne, 2019.

———. *Why Christianity Must Change or Die.* San Francisco: HarperOne, 1999.

Thiemann, Ronald F. *Religion in Public Life: A Dilemma for Democracy.* Washington, DC: Georgetown University Press, 1996.

Thomas Aquinas. *On Kingship.* In *From Irenaeus to Grotius: A Sourcebook of Christian Political Thought 100–1625,* edited by Oliver O'Donovan and Joan Lockwood O'Donovan, 330–54. Grand Rapids: Eerdmans, 1999.

Townes, Emilie M. *Womanist Ethics and the Cultural Production of Evil.* New York: Palgrave Macmillan, 2006.

U.S. Conference of Catholic Bishops. *Economic Justice for All: A Pastoral Letter on Catholic Social Teaching and the U.S. Economy.* 1986.

Volf, Miroslav. "The Gift of Infertility." *The Christian Century* 122:12 (2005) 33.

Weber, Max. *The Protestant Ethic and the Spirit of Capitalism, and Other Writings.* Edited by Peter Baehr and Gordon C. Wells. London: Penguin, 2002.

White, Lynn, Jr. "The Historical Roots of Our Ecologic Crisis." *Science* 155 (1967) 1203–7.

Winthrop, John. "A Model of Christian Charity." In *The Puritans in America: A Narrative Anthology,* edited by Alan Heimert and Andrew Delbanco, 81–92. Cambridge: Harvard University Press, 1985.

Wootson, Cleve R., Jr. "Rev. William Barber Builds a Moral Movement." *The Washington Post,* June 29, 2017. https://www.washingtonpost.com/news/acts-of-faith/wp/2017/06/29/woe-unto-those-who-legislate-evil-rev-william-barber-builds-a-moral-movement/.

Zauzmer, Julie. "Trump Uttered What Many Supporters Consider Blasphemy. Here's Why Most Will Probably Forgive Him." *Washington Post,* September 14, 2019. https://www.washingtonpost.com/politics/trump-uttered-what-many-supporters-consider-blasphemy-heres-why-most-will-probably-forgive-him/2019/09/13/685c0bce-d64f-11e9-9343-40db57cf6abd_story.html.